Real Security

Protecting America and
Restoring Our Leadership in the World

CONTENTS

Produced by the Senate and House Democrats

Iraq

Tab 1: Issue Overview

Tab 2: Additional Resources
★ Text of the United States Policy on Iraq Act Amendment
★ *Progress in Iraq*, Center for American Progress, 3/20/06
★ List of additional resources

Tab 3: State-by-State-Data
★ Service Members in Iraq and Afghanistan, By State

Energy Independence

Tab 1: Issue Overview

Tab 2: Additional Resources
★ List of additional resources

Real Security
The Democratic Plan to Protect America and Restore Our Leadership in the World

March 29, 2006, 109th Congress, Second Session

The first responsibility of our government is the security of every American. In this era of unprecedented and unpredictable challenge, we must be prepared for any threat.

The men and women of America's armed forces and those on the front lines here at home have met every challenge with skill, bravery, and selfless dedication. They, along with veterans, military retirees and the families of those who have given their lives or have been wounded in defense of our country, deserve the gratitude and support of the American people. We will always honor their service and fulfill our promises to them.

We believe America is best protected, and freedom best advanced, by national security policies -- including homeland, energy, and diplomatic strategies -- that are both tough <u>and</u> smart.

Democrats offer a plan for **Real Security** to rebuild our military; equip and train our first responders and others on the front lines here at home; provide needed benefits to our troops and veterans; fully man and equip our National Guard; promote alternative fuels and reduce dependence on foreign oil; and, restore Americans' confidence in their government's ability to respond in the face of a terrorist attack or natural disaster.

To protect the American people, we will immediately implement the recommendations of the independent bipartisan 9/11 Commission and finally protect our ports and airports, our borders, mass transit systems, our chemical and nuclear power plants, and our food and water supplies from terrorist attack.

After September 11, all Americans trusted President Bush to take the steps necessary to keep our country safe. Since then, inadequate planning and incompetent policies have failed to make Americans as safe as we should be.

The tragedy of Hurricane Katrina showed that the federal government was still not prepared to respond.

Under President Bush and the Republican majority in Congress, the war in Iraq began with manipulated intelligence and no plan for success; our ports and other critical infrastructure remain vulnerable, while both soldiers in the field and first responders at home lack the basic equipment and resources they were promised. Both in the Persian Gulf and our own Gulf Coast, lucrative no-bid contracts have gone to companies such as Halliburton, Kellogg, Brown and Root, and others with friends in high places and records of cheating taxpayers. And despite record high fuel prices, our country remains heavily dependent on foreign oil because of an energy policy that benefits the big oil interests.

Americans want and deserve change. Democrats' plan for **Real Security** will protect Americans and restore our country's position of international leadership.

Real Security

21st Century Military
To Ensure Unparalleled Military Strength and Honor our Troops, we will:
- Rebuild a state-of-the-art military by making the needed investments in equipment and manpower so that we can project power to protect America wherever and whenever necessary.
- Guarantee that our troops have the protective gear, equipment, and training they need and are never sent to war without accurate intelligence and a strategy for success.
- Enact a GI Bill of Rights for the 21st Century that guarantees our troops -- active, reserve, and retired -- our veterans, and their families receive the pay, health care, mental health services, and other benefits they have earned and deserve.
- Strengthen the National Guard, in partnership with the nation's Governors, to ensure it is fully manned, equipped and available to meet missions at home and abroad.

War on Terror
To Defeat Terrorists and Stop the Spread of Weapons of Mass Destruction, we will:
- Eliminate Osama Bin Laden, destroy terrorist networks like al Qaeda, finish the job in Afghanistan and end the threat posed by the Taliban.

- Double the size of our Special Forces, increase our human intelligence capabilities, and ensure our intelligence is free from political pressure.
- Eliminate terrorist breeding grounds by combating the economic, social, and political conditions that allow extremism to thrive; lead international efforts to uphold and defend human rights; and renew longstanding alliances that have advanced our national security objectives.
- Secure by 2010 loose nuclear materials that terrorists could use to build nuclear weapons or "dirty bombs."
- Redouble efforts to stop nuclear weapons development in Iran and North Korea.

Homeland Security
To Protect America from Terrorism and Natural Disasters, we will:
- Immediately implement the recommendations of the independent, bipartisan 9/11 Commission including securing national borders, ports, airports and mass transit systems.
- Screen 100% of containers and cargo bound for the U.S. in ships or airplanes at the point of origin and safeguard America's nuclear and chemical plants, and food and water supplies.
- Prevent outsourcing of critical components of our national security infrastructure -- such as ports, airports and mass transit -- to foreign interests that put America at risk.
- Provide firefighters, emergency medical workers, police officers, and other workers on the front lines with the training, staffing, equipment and cutting-edge technology they need.
- Protect America from biological terrorism and pandemics, including the Avian flu, by investing in the public health infrastructure and training public health workers.

Iraq
To Honor the Sacrifice of Our Troops, we will:
- Ensure 2006 is a year of significant transition to full Iraqi sovereignty, with the Iraqis assuming primary responsibility for securing and governing their country and with the responsible redeployment of U.S. forces.
- Insist that Iraqis make the political compromises necessary to unite their country and defeat the insurgency; promote regional diplomacy; and strongly encourage our allies and other nations to play a constructive role.
- Hold the Bush Administration accountable for its manipulated pre-war intelligence, poor planning and contracting abuses that have placed our troops at greater risk and wasted billions of taxpayer dollars.

Energy Independence
To Free America from Dependence on Foreign Oil, we will:
- Achieve energy independence for America by 2020 by eliminating reliance on oil from the Middle East and other unstable regions of the world.

- Increase production of alternate fuels from America's heartland including bio-fuels, geothermal, clean coal, fuel cells, solar and wind; promote hybrid and flex fuel vehicle technology and manufacturing; enhance energy efficiency and conservation incentives.

Real Security:
Protecting America and Restoring Our Leadership in the World

21st CENTURY MILITARY

America has the finest military in the world. But since 9/11, our nation's armed forces have become over-extended and some recruiting goals have not been met. Because of the Bush Administration's poor planning, many units are on their second or even third tour in Iraq or Afghanistan and Army and Marine Corps personnel still do not have adequate body armor or sufficiently armored vehicles. We are committed to ensuring that the United States military remains second to none.

The men and women of America's armed forces and first responders here at home have met every challenge with skill, bravery and selfless dedication. They, along with veterans, military retirees and the families of those who have given their lives in defense of our country, deserve the gratitude and support of the American people. We will always honor their service and fulfill our promises to them.

To Ensure Unparalleled Military Strength and Honor our Troops, Democrats will:

- Rebuild a state-of-the-art military by making the needed investments in equipment and manpower so that we can project power to protect America wherever and whenever necessary.

- Guarantee that our troops have the protective gear, equipment, and training they need and are never sent to war without accurate intelligence and a strategy for success.

- Enact a GI Bill of Rights for the 21st Century that guarantees our troops -- active, reserve, and retired -- our veterans, and their families receive the pay, health care, mental health services, and other benefits they have earned and deserve.

- Strengthen the National Guard, in partnership with the nation's Governors, to ensure it is fully manned, equipped and available to meet missions at home and abroad.

Bush/Republican Record on Military & Veterans' Issues

Our military is second to none, and our troops are serving heroically. And yet, the Bush Administration's poor planning and incompetence has put dangerous strains on our troops, while leaving them inadequately equipped and vulnerable. At the same time, the Administration has failed to live up to their promises to our veterans who have already valiantly served this nation. The Bush Administration failed to predict the need for equipment and gear to protect our troops, failed to budget for the health care needs of returning soldiers, and has refused to provide promised benefits to military families and disabled veterans.

Failed to fully equip and protect our soldiers. After three years at war in Iraq, thousands of Army and Marine Corps personnel still do not have adequate body armor or sufficient armor for their military transport vehicles. For example, about half of the Army's 20,000 Humvees have improvised shielding that typically leaves the underside vulnerable to remotely detonated bombs. An untold number of soldiers and their families have been force to purchase body armor – to ensure they had necessary protection when in Iraq -- so many in fact that Congress passed a law requiring the DoD to reimburse soldiers for these items. And equipment problems are more severe for the National Guard and Reserve. In 2005, the Army Reserve reported it had only about 76 percent of the equipment it requires, with as much as 44 percent of its equipment needing servicing. [*GAO*, "An Integrated Plan is Needed to Address Army Reserve Personnel and Equipment Shortages." Rpt # GAO-05-660, 7/12/05] A Pentagon study suggests 80 percent of Marine fatalities caused by bullet wounds to the torso were likely preventable. [*New York Times*, 1/6/06] Our soldiers and their families have paid a price for the Bush Administration's lack of preparedness.

Army stretched too thin. Another cost of the Bush Administration's failure to plan properly for the war in Iraq is that the Army has been stretched by frequent troop rotations. Many units are on their second or even third tour in Iraq or Afghanistan without adequate time in rotation at home to rest and recuperate. At least 40 percent of deployed personnel are from the Guard and Reserve. Nearly all of the available combat units in the U.S. Army, Army National Guard, and Marine Corps have been used in Iraq and Afghanistan. Before the war started, Eric Shinskei, Chief of Staff for the Army, stated "Something on the order of several hundred thousand soldiers are probably, you know, a figure that would be required." [Testimony before the Senate Armed Services Committee, 2/25/2003] A recent report prepared for the Pentagon concluded that the Army has become a "thin green line" that could snap unless relief comes soon. [Report by Andrew Krepenevich, Thin Green Line, 1/06]

Cuts National Guard by 17,000. Despite recent reports of the tremendous strain that the Iraq and Afghanistan War have placed on our troops, the President's budget fails to fund the force size authorized by law. The budget would fund 17,100 fewer Army National Guard and 5,000 fewer Army Reserves than are authorized by law. The National Guard is a cost-effective, capable combat force in the war on terror and an essential state partner in responding to domestic disasters and emergencies. As the National Guard Association stated, "the very idea that a reduction in strength of reserve components so fully involved in current operations and projected as the linchpin for future operations, both overseas and in the defense and security of the homeland, is ludicrous." [Letter to Senator John Warner, 12/12/05]

The Bush Administration defense strategy fails to live up to the increasing threats. The Defense Department's strategy document, the Quadrennial Defense Review, says our military must be able to take on even more missions to face future threats. Yet the Bush Administration support neither the number of troops nor the force structure to allow us to meet them. The Bush Administration stated last year they needed 77 Army combat brigades, now they say they need

70. Further, the Defense Department's strategy reduces the Air Force by 40,000 and the Navy by more than 12,000.

President's budget fails to include $21 billion in requested military needs – the largest amount denied since 9/11. The President's fiscal year 2007 budget fails to include requested equipment totaling more than $7 billion for the Army, $4.5 billion for the Navy, $5.6 billion for the Air Force, $2.5 billion for the Marine Corps, and $1.61billion for the National Guard. The Army is requesting $450 million for unmet depot maintenance needs to repair the equipment broken during combat operations in Iraq and Afghanistan. [Rep. Skelton press release, 3/3/06]

Bush Administration cuts off veterans' health care, but still have growing need with veterans returning from Iraq and Afghanistan. In January 2003, the Bush Administration cut off VA health care for 164,000 veterans without service-connected disabilities, who make as little as $25,000 a year. Over the past three years, this has prevented 1 million veterans, who make as little as $26,903, from enrolling in VA health care. As of December 2005, VA had treated more than 144,000 of the 505,366 veterans from Operation Iraqi Freedom and Enduring Freedom. [VA, 2/14/06]

Voted for $28 billion in cuts in veterans= benefits and health care. In FY 2004, House Republicans voted to cut $14 billion from veterans= benefits, including veterans= pension, compensation, education and other benefits, and another $14 billion from veterans= health care. [*H Con. Res 95*, Vote #82, 3/21/03]

Bush Administration shortchanged veterans' health, because it failed to budget for returning veterans. In the summer of 2005, the Bush Administration acknowledged a $2.7 billion shortfall in veterans health care funding -- a deficiency that Democrats had been pointing out for several years. The Bush team sent hundreds of thousands of Americans to war but failed to anticipate that they would need medical care when they came home. According to the Bush Administration's Secretary of Veterans Affairs, his department failed to budget for 77,000 new veterans entering the VA medical system. [Testimony of Secretary of Veterans Affairs before Senate Veterans Affairs Committee, 6/28/05] There are early warning signs that the Bush Administration has once again failed to anticipate the demand for services from returning veterans, particularly the need for mental health services. [VA 2/14/06; VA 2/7/06]

Veterans facing higher fees. As a result of Bush Administration proposals, those who use the VA health care system are facing substantially higher co-payments, and waiting times, and are at-risk for higher fees. [The Independent Budget, Critical Issues Report for Fiscal Year 2007; Veterans Institute for Security and Democracy, Review of Veterans Funding, 11/30/05] For the fourth year in a row, the President's budget proposes raises health care costs for 1 million veterans by imposing new fees costing them more than $2.6 billion over five years, and driving at least 200,000 veterans out of the system.

Investments in veterans' health care still fall short. This year's President's budget "plan has come up short of what's needed to honor America's commitment to veterans," according to the Disabled American Veterans. [Press release, 2/9/06] Because Democrats succeeded in investing more for veterans' health care last year, the President's budget provides about $3 billion more than last year. However, it still remains $1 billion less than veterans' service organizations specify is needed, and is $10 billion below the amount needed to maintain services at current levels over the next five years.

President's Budget increases health care costs for military retirees by as much as $1,000 per year. The President's budget increases TRICARE health care premiums for 3 to 4 million of the nation's military retirees under 65 and their family members. Under the new Bush Administration proposals, health care premiums will double for senior enlisted retirees and triple for officer retirees by 2008 and drug co-payments will increase. This initiative to tax military retirees will save the Defense Department $11.2 billion over five years by raising costs to families -- driving military retirees out of the system altogether and leaving them without the health care they earned through at least 20 years of service.

Bush Administration has opposed living up to our promises to veterans, military retirees, and their families. In 2003, the Bush Administration threatened to veto the entire defense authorization bill if it included a provision to end the "Disabled Veterans Tax," which has forced disabled military retirees to lose one dollar of their military retirement pay for each dollar of VA service-connected compensation for a service-connected disability. The Administration opposed ending the Widow's Tax, which cut benefits to the survivors of military retirees age 62 and older.

Democratic Record on Military & Veterans' Issues

Democrats are committed to strengthening our military and honoring those who have served this country. That is why we have worked to guarantee that our troops have the equipment they need and drafted a New GI Bill of Rights for the 21st Century. This package would improve benefits for our men and women in uniform today and provide long overdue benefits for the veterans and military retirees who have already served. It would improve veterans' health care, including mental health care, to meet the needs of our returning troops.

Democrats have been fighting to make sure our troops are fully equipped. Every step along the way, Democrats have sought to ensure that our troops were fully equipped for the war in Iraq. For example, because of Democratic efforts, the 2003 Iraqi supplemental included more funds for HUMVEEs, body armor, and jammers to prevent the detonation of explosive devises. Democrats offered amendments to shift $322 million from reconstruction to safety equipment for U.S. troops in Iraq (Sen. Dodd) and to shift $4.6 billion from Iraqi reconstruction to support and safety for our troops including critical funding for repairing and replacing the critical equipment for combat in Iraq (Rep. Obey). However, both of these efforts were rejected by Republicans. [RC 376, S.Amdt. 1817 to S. 1689, 49-37, 10/2/03; H.R. 3289, House Vote #547, 10/16/03. Rejected 209-216] Democrats succeeded in requiring the Defense Department to reimburse service members for the cost of any protective, safety or health equipment purchased by them or their families. [RC 112, S.Amdt. 3312 to S.2400, 91-0, 6/14/04] More recently, Democrats succeeded in providing an additional $213 million to the army for the procurement of up-armored high mobility multipurpose-wheeled vehicles, known as Humvees. [RC 108, S.Amdt. 520 to S. 1268, 61-39, 4/21/05]

Fighting to Make Health Care Accessible and Affordable for Our Veterans. The war has produced a greater need for veterans' health care. As of December 2005, VA had treated more than 144,000 of the 505,366 veterans of Operation Iraqi Freedom and Enduring Freedom. [VA, 2/14/06] In 2003, Democrats prevented huge cuts approved by House Republicans. In 2004, we succeeded in forcing a $1 billion increase over the President's request. In 2005, Democrats called for an additional $3 billion over the President's budget and forced the Bush Administration to acknowledge that it had failed to budget for returning veterans. [HRes 95, Vote #82, 3/17/2005; Failed 180-242; R 3-218; D 176-24; I 1-0] This year, Senate Republicans rejected a Democratic amendment to make veterans health care funding mandatory to ensure that the growing health care needs of America's veterans are met. [RC 63, S.Amdt. 3141 to S.Con.Res. 83, 45-55, 3/16/06] Senate Republicans also rejected a Democratic amendment to add $1.5 billion for VA health care and reject increased fees and copayments for veterans. [RC 41, S.Amdt. 3007 to S.Con.Res. 83, 46-54, 3/14/06] And House Republicans have denied a fair vote on adding $630 million to provide urgently needed health care for troops returning from Iraq and Afghanistan in the Iraq Supplemental spending bill. [HR.4939, Vote #40, 3/15/2006; Blocked 224-192]

Fighting to Meet Mental Health Needs of Returning Troops. With up to one-third of Iraq war veterans may be suffering from some degree of Post Traumatic Stress Disease, Democrats are fighting to meet the needs of these returning veterans. [UPI, 1/27/06] For example, Democrats sought to provide an additional $500 million per year for the next five years for mental health services for veterans, but Republicans rejected that effort [RC 343, Boxer Amdt. 2634 to S.2020, 43-55, 11/17/05] In the House, Democrats, as part of the New GI Bill of Rights, have proposed to improve mental health support for returning soldiers (HR 1588) through enhanced education and outreach, improved screening, and effective treatment and counseling for veterans and family members.

Succeeded in Extending Health Care to National Guard and Reservists. Recognizing their unprecedented sacrifice in the Iraq War, Democrats have fought to extend health care for National Guard and reservists. [*RC 81*, Lincoln. Amdt. to S.Con.Res. 23, 46-51, 3/25/03] Republicans have rejected efforts to expand TRICARE eligibility, but Democratic pressure resulted in reservists being able to enroll in TRICARE if they do not have employer-sponsored health insurance, and in reservists being eligible for medical care for 6 months, after being released from from active duty. In 2004, Democrats succeeded in providing one year of TRICARE benefits for every 90 days of service for activated Reservists. But we continue to fight to provide full TRICARE benefits to all members of the Guard and Reserve and their families, for an affordable monthly premium. The Senate has passed this critical provision, but Republicans in the House opposed expanding TRICARE to thousands of National Guard & Reserve volunteers. [*RC 105*, S.Amdt. 3258 to S. 2400, 70-25, 6/2/04; HR 1815, Vote #221, 5/25/2005; Failed 211-218; R 9-218; D 201-0; I 1-0]

Fighting against increases in health care costs for military retirees. The President's budget increases TRICARE health care premiums for 3-4 million of the nation's military retirees under 65 and their family members. Premiums will double for senior enlisted retirees and triple for officer retirees by 2008 and drug co-payments will increase. A Democratic amendment to the Senate budget resolution allowed for increased funding for retirees TRICARE to be paid for by eliminating certain tax breaks. [*RC 67*, S.Amdt. 3143 to S.Con.Res. 83, 46-53, 3/16/06] House Democratic Leaders sent a letter urging President Bush to rethink increasing the costs of veterans' health care and Rep. Edwards has introduced legislation to prohibit the increases. [letter, 1/25/06; H.R. 4949]

Succeeded in making military pay increases permanent. In 2003, Democrats led the fight to make the increase in imminent danger pay and the family separation allowance permanent– over the opposition of the Bush Administration.

Fighting to end the Military Families Tax. The Survivor Benefit Plan penalizes survivors, many of them widows of those killed in combat. These widows lose their survivor benefits if they also receive Dependency and Indemnity Compensation (DIC) from the VA because their spouse has died of a service-connected injury. Democrats are working to end the Military Families Tax for the 53,000 spouses, despite Republican opposition in the House to even having the issue considered. [*RC 307*, S.Amdt. 2424 to S. 1042, 92-6, 11/8/05; HR 1815, House Vote #212, 5/25/2005; Blocked 225-200; R 225-0; D 0-199; I 0-1] That is why House Democrats have led the fight to force a vote on the H.R.808 through a discharge petition.

Fighting to End the Disabled Veterans Tax. Democrats have been fighting to end the disabled veterans' tax, which forces disabled military retirees to give up one dollar of their military pension for every dollar of VA disability pay they receive. Because of Democratic pressure, a Republican compromise was enacted, but it takes ten years to eliminate the tax while requiring two-thirds of military retirees with service-connected disabilities to continue to pay it. Republicans rejected Democratic efforts to end the tax immediately. [*H.R. 1588*, Vote # 616, 11/7/03. Rejected 188-217 (R 4-215; D 183-2)] Democrats continue to work to end this unfair tax for all of the nearly 400,000 military retirees who are affected by it, and have offered a discharge petition to force a vote on the bipartisan H.R. 303, the Retired Pay Restoration Act of 2005.

Succeeded in ending the Widow's Tax. Democrats have fought to restore full military survivor benefits to the survivors of military retirees age 62 and older. This effort succeeded in getting the Widow's Tax (SBP provision) phased out in the final Defense Authorization bill in 2004, over Bush Administration opposition.

Rhetoric vs. Reality on Military & Veterans' Issues

Rhetoric: **Any time we've got folks in harm's way, they deserve the best: the best pay possible, the best training possible and the best equipment possible. It's a commitment this administration has made since I've been the commander in chief and it's a commitment we will keep."** [President Bush Discusses Progress in War on Terror to National Guard, 2/9/06]

Reality: One month after the war began, the Pentagon stopped ordering body armor – bringing about chronic shortages and forcing soldiers to buy them on their own. [*New York Times*, 3/7/05] In January 2006, more than one year after Congress passed legislation requiring the Pentagon to reimburse these soldiers for body armor purchases, it has only just begun implementing this critical program. Our soldiers and their families have paid a price for the Administration's lack of preparedness. A Pentagon study suggests 80 percent of Marine fatalities caused by bullet wounds to the torso were likely preventable. [*New York Times*, 1/6/06]

Rhetoric: **"We have made health care a top priority for my administration. With my 2007 budget, we will increase the VA Benefit since 2001. Our increased funding has given almost a million more veterans access to the V.A. Medical care system."** [President Bush, 2/24/06]

Reality: **The Bush Budget Falls Short on Veterans' Healthcare.** According to veterans' advocacy groups, Bush's VA budget falls about $1.3 billion short of what is needed for medical care, given the increasing demand for services and the rising cost of care and basic operating costs. [Disabled Veterans press release, February 8, 2006]

Reality: **Bush Budget Will Make Military Retirees Pay More.** "The Bush administration wants many military retirees to pay more for health care, a proposal that could force the Republican-run Congress to choose between savvy politics and budget discipline… To help contain those costs, President Bush's proposal includes higher prescription drug co-payments for all beneficiaries of military health care except those on active duty, and increased annual enrollment fees for military retirees under age 65." [USA Today, 2/21/06]

Rhetoric: **"We must …stand behind the American military." President's State of the Union 2006**

Reality: Our soldiers in Iraq have not been getting all of the equipment they need to successfully complete their mission. Two new reports show that, under Bush, the Army is overstretched and under enormous strain. There are numerous recruiting problems and a weakened National Guard and Reserve.

Rhetoric: **"We are grateful to all who volunteer to wear our nation's uniform." President's State of the Union 2006**

Reality: The Bush Administration's cost-cutting decisions have denied VA health care to more than 260,000 veterans. Republicans have refused to end the disabled veterans' tax for two-thirds of disabled military retirees and rejected providing military health care for all reservists for a low fee.

Critics of the Bush/Republican Record on
Military & Veterans' Issues

On Troop Shortages

"All of this fuss — whether it be (extended deployments) or having sufficient armor — all of this is a continuation of the issue of poor planning ... lack of understanding of the consequences of invading Iraq,"

> Retired Maj. Gen. Nash, an analyst with the Council on Foreign Relations
> CBS, War Readiness Again Hot Issue, 12/9/04

"I think there was dereliction in insufficient forces being put on the ground and fully understanding the military dimensions of the plan. I think there was dereliction in lack of planning."

> Gen. Anthony Zinni and Tom Clancy
> Battle Ready

"...the Army finds itself severely undermanned -- cut to 10 active divisions but asked by the administration to support a foreign policy that requires at least 12 or 14."

> Paul Eaton, Retired Army major general
> *New York Times*, A Top-Down Review for the Pentagon, 3/19/06

We have a force in Iraq that's much too small to stabilize the situation. It's about half the size, or maybe even a third, of what we need.

> Gen. Merrill "Tony" McPeak, *Air Force chief of staff, 1990-94*
> *Rolling Stone*, The Generals Speak, 11/3/04

National Guard Cuts

"This is a formula for disaster,"

> Governor Dirk Kempthorne.
> *Washington Post*, Governors Challenge Cuts In National Guard Funds, 2/26/06

Increase in TRICARE Health Fees for Military Retirees

"Don't try to tell us that a country that can afford hundreds of billions of dollars in pork spending and tax cuts can't afford to pay for both military weapons and retiree health care."

> Steve Strobridge, retired Air Force Colonel and government relations director for the Military Officers Association of America. [*Army Times*, Hikes Proposed in Tricare Costs for Retirees, 1/26/06]

Real Security:
Protecting America and Restoring Our Leadership in the World

Summary: *The U.S. Military: Under Strain and At Risk* **by the National Security Advisory Group, January 2006**

By failing to adequately plan for post-conflict Iraq, failing to send enough forces to accomplish the mission with an acceptable level of risk, and failing to adequately equip the Americans sent into harm's way, the Bush Administration has put our ground troops under enormous strain that, if not soon relieved, will have "highly-corrosive and potentially long-term effects on the force."

The report lays out five recommended courses of action to prepare for future military needs:

1. **Fully fund the post-Iraq recovery and transformation of our ground forces.**

2. **Adapt the National Guard and Reserves for the future.**

3. **Increase the deployable Army forces by at least 30,000 personnel.**

4. **Rebalance U.S. military capabilities for 21st century missions such as combating terrorism and insurgency and conducting reconstruction operations.**

5. **Increase support for recruiting and retention efforts.**

The U.S. Military: Under Strain and at Risk
A paper for the National Security Advisory Group II
Executive Summary

In the current debate over Iraq, there is an elephant in the room that few are willing to acknowledge. While the U.S. military has performed superbly in Afghanistan, Iraq and elsewhere, our ground forces are under enormous strain. This strain, if not soon relieved, will have highly corrosive and potentially long-term effects on the force.

We believe that the Bush administration has broken faith with the American soldier and Marine:
- by failing to plan adequately for post-conflict operations in Iraq;
- by failing to send enough forces to accomplish that mission at an acceptable level of risk; and
- by failing to adequately equip and protect the young Americans they sent into harm's way.

These failures have created a real risk of "breaking the force" – a force that is critical to protecting and advancing our national interests, now and in the future. The American military deserves better. The American people deserve better.

This paper is intended to sound a warning – to raise awareness about the state of our ground forces today and the very real risk that poses to our future security. This paper also proposes an action plan for restoring the health and vitality of the U.S. military. The administration has under discussion some of what is recommended here, but the actions actually being taken fall far short of what is required.

The Facts

- *Nearly all of the available combat units in the U.S. Army, Army National Guard and Marine Corps have been used in current operations.* Every available combat brigade from the active duty Army has already been to Afghanistan or Iraq at least once for a 12 month tour. Many are now in their second or third tours of duty. Approximately 95% the Army National Guard's combat battalions and special operations units have been mobilized since 9/11. Short of full mobilization or a new Presidential declaration of national emergency, there is little available combat capacity remaining in the Army National Guard. All active duty Marine Corps units are being used on a "tight" rotation schedule – seven months deployed, less than a year home to reset, and then another seven months deployed – and all of its Reserve combat units have been mobilized.

- *The Army is experiencing the beginnings of what could become a major <u>recruiting</u> crisis.* At the end of FY2005, the active Army fell 6,627 recruits short of its annual goal of 80,000 new accessions. Although this shortfall is not alarming in and of itself, there are some important indicators that the recruiting shortfall will be far larger next year. In addition, some worry that the Army is lowering its quality standards, drawing a higher than normal percentage of its new recruits from "Category IV" (the lowest aptitude level accepted). This year will be critical in determining whether the active Army is simply going through a bad patch or entering one of the worst recruiting crises in its history. Meanwhile, the Army Reserve fell 16% behind its recruiting target for the year, and the Guard 20% short of its annual goal.

- *The Army and Marine Corps are meeting their overall retention goals, for the moment, but some fear a major <u>retention</u> crisis may be looming for the Army.* While the Army met its overall retention goals in 2005, the Army National Guard and Army Reserve fell short of their goals for those deciding whether to renew their commitment for the first time, creating the potential for long-term imbalances in the force. In addition, some of our most highly skilled people, like Special Operations Forces, are leaving the force to become more highly paid contractors. Furthermore, between 2001 and 2004, divorce rates and the incidence of domestic violence increased markedly, indicating the severity of the strains on Army personnel and their families. Some commanders fear that these seemingly unrelated developments could auger a retention crisis in the future.

- *The Army and the Army National Guard have experienced critical <u>equipment shortfalls</u> that increased the level of risk to forces deployed in Iraq and Afghanistan and reduced the readiness of units in the United States.* From the beginning of the Iraq war until as late as last year, the active Army experienced shortages of key equipment for deployed troops. While many of these shortfalls have been addressed, the readiness ratings of many non-deployed units, including some slated to deploy later this year, have dropped to very low levels. This situation is even worse for Army National Guard units. These readiness shortfalls are only likely to grow as the war in Iraq continues to accelerate the wearout rate of all categories of equipment for the ground forces.

The Risks

- *The Army and the Marine Corps cannot sustain today's operational tempo indefinitely without doing real damage to their forces.*

- *If recruiting trends do not improve over the next year, the Army, both active and reserve, will experience great difficulty fully manning its planned force structure and providing the needed rotation base for operations in Iraq and Afghanistan.* Fewer than needed recruits and first-term reenlistees could result in a significant "hollowing" and imbalance in the Army. There is already a deficit of some 18,000 personnel in the Army's junior enlisted grades. Even if it meets its recruiting and retention goals, the Army is expected to be short some 30K soldiers (not including stop loss) by the end of FY06. This will undermine unit readiness, exacerbate PERSTEMPO strains, and jeopardize the Army's ability to populate its planned force structure. These factors will create tremendous internal pressures to begin drawing down the level of Army forces in Iraq by next spring, whatever the conditions on the ground may be.

- *If retention rates decline significantly, the viability of the All Volunteer force could be threatened.* The All Volunteer Force is now in historically uncharted waters: fighting a protracted conflict with volunteers rather than draftees. The conventional wisdom is that while most will stay in the force after one or even two tours, there is a real concern that a third deployment in a compressed time period may cause many to choose to leave the force.

- *In the meantime, the United States has only limited ground force capability ready to respond to other contingencies. The absence of a credible strategic reserve in our ground forces increases the risk that potential adversaries will be tempted to challenge the United States.* Although the United States can still deploy air, naval, and other more specialized assets to deter or respond to aggression, the visible overextension of our ground forces could weaken our ability to deter aggression.

- *Resetting, recapitalizing and modernizing our nation's ground forces will be no small challenge and will require substantial and sustained investment.* Severe wear and tear on Army, Marine Corps and Guard equipment is increasing the costs of "resetting" the force as units return home. In addition, the costs associated with recapitalizing aging forces and transforming for new missions are only increasing.

The Way Ahead

Timely action is required to preserve the All Volunteer Force, help our ground forces recover fully from the strains of current operations, and rebalance and transform our military to meet the challenges of the 21st century. Obviously, much will depend on the size of deployments in Iraq for the next year or two. Those deployments will be influenced by the state of the ground forces, but should be determined by the situation in the ground in Iraq. But as our forces draw down in Iraq, the nation must pursue five courses of action to prepare for future military requirements:

1. Fully fund the recovery and transformation of our nation's ground forces.

In order to restore the health of U.S. ground forces in the wake of Iraq, we must invest substantial resources to reset, recapitalize, and modernize the force.

Resetting the force is underway and has been funded through emergency supplemental appropriations. But anticipated equipment rehabilitation costs may extend beyond the supplemental appropriations for Iraq and Afghanistan, which could leave both the Army and the Marine Corps with big unpaid bills. Congress must ensure that even when supplemental funding ends, adequate funding for resetting the force continues. Without this, neither service will be able to "get well" in the wake of Iraq.

In addition, both the Army and the Marine Corps have systems that are nearing the end of their projected service lives. Soon they will need to embark on major recapitalization programs to keep their forces supplied with reliable, functioning equipment. Further, both the Army and the Marine Corps have ambitious plans to modernize and transform their forces to execute 21st century missions.

2. Adapt the roles, missions, organization, training and equipment of the National Guard and Reserves for the future.

Since the end of the Cold War, and especially in the aftermath of 9/11, the National Guard and Reserves have evolved from being a strategic reserve – forces to be mobilized for a major war or national emergency -- to an operational reserve – forces that regularly support the operations of the active duty military at home and abroad.

The reality is that the operational reserve model is here to stay. Demand for U.S. military forces is likely to remain high (even if not as high as today) and budget, demographic and recruiting realities will preclude a major expansion of the active duty military in the near term. But this new reality is not reflected in how reserve forces are being organized, trained, equipped, and funded. Consequently, we have a legacy force making heroic efforts to perform a new set of missions at an unsustainable tempo of operations and without the necessary resources, training and equipment.

We need a new social compact between the U.S. government and our "citizen soldiers" that clarifies both the new expectations of a more operational reserve and the government's obligations to those who are serving under this new construct. We must preserve this essential link between the military and the body politic – to ensure that any President is able to mobilize substantial numbers of America's citizen soldiers when necessary. Given that future demand is like to span a broad range of missions – from high-intensity combat operations and stability and reconstruction operations to counterterrorism and homeland defense – we need to prepare and resource reserve forces that are capable of conducting a wide variety of operations. In particular, homeland defense and civil support are becoming increasingly important missions for the National Guard, and that should be reflected in how some units of the Guard are equipped and trained.

3. Increase the pool of deployable forces in the Army over time by at least 30,000 personnel.

Looking to the future, demand for U.S. ground forces will most likely remain higher than pre-9/11 levels. We should make permanent the 30,000 person increase in active duty Army end strength that the Congress has authorized but that the Secretary of Defense views as only a temporary measure. Making this increase permanent would enable the Army to grow its active duty force structure to at least 48 brigade combat teams (rather than just 42) over time.

While increasing the size of the Army would make it easier to meet future operational requirements, it will certainly not be easy. In the near term, recruiting additional soldiers will be difficult, if not impossible – at least until we turn the corner in Iraq. Building additional force structure will take time, both to establish new units and to populate them with trained personnel. Increasing force structure will also be expensive – about $1.5 billion for each new brigade plus recurring personnel costs.

4. Rebalance the mix of U.S. military capabilities for 21st century missions.

Throughout the post-Cold War period, and increasingly since 9/11, the U.S. military has experienced a mismatch between the capabilities it inherited from the Cold War and the capabilities it needs to deal with emerging threats. Forces optimized to fight major conventional wars are now being asked to combat terrorism, conduct stability and reconstruction operations, and fight counterinsurgency campaigns. The mix of capabilities resident in the force needs to be fundamentally rebalanced. This requires four parallel efforts:

- First, the U.S. military must convert units that are in low demand in the new security environment into unit types that are in high demand in order to reduce the most acute strains on the force. That is already underway, but should be accelerated.

- Second, we need to rebalance the mix of capabilities in the active and reserve components and create more stable and predictable schedules for deployment.

- Third, we need to take maximum advantage of technology and services offered by the private sector to make the best use of our military personnel. In today's military, incorporating the latest information technology and "working smarter" can substantially reduce manpower requirements.

- More broadly, the U.S. government needs to build deployable operational capacity in key civilian agencies like the State Department to conduct critical tasks for which the U.S. military does not have a comparative advantage. The U.S. also needs to encourage the development of greater international capacity to conduct complex missions like stabilization and reconstruction.

5. Increase support for recruiting and retention efforts.

Although President Bush has sent the U.S. military to war in Iraq and to fight terrorism around the globe, he has failed to mobilize the American people for either cause. There has been no JFK-like "ask not what your country can do for you, but what you can do for your country" speech – no call to national service. This failure of leadership has only widened the gap between U.S. military personnel and the American people they are risking their lives to protect and contributes to the recruiting crisis.

Congress should continue to give the military services the flexibility they need to tailor and target recruiting and retention incentives to be as effective as possible. The

2006 National Defense Authorization Act includes a wide variety of incentives, from higher cash bonuses to education benefits to down payment assistance for first homes to referral bonuses for serving soldiers who bring in new recruits.

Additionally, we should offer a broader range of options to young Americans who are interested in serving their country. It should be easier for people to transition back and forth between active duty service and the Guard or reserves, easier for "middle aged" Americans to join the military, easier for those who leave the military to come back into service, and easier to bring civilians with critical skill sets into some form of voluntary national service.

Conclusion

The strains on the U.S. Army and Marine Corps are serious and growing, and the viability of our All Volunteer Force is at risk. To guarantee U.S. national security, we must keep faith with the men and women in our military and with the American people. We need to act now to protect and restore our armed forces.

The U.S. Military Under Strain and at Risk
A paper by the National Security Advisory Group II

Introduction

Today, in operations from Iraq and Afghanistan to southeast Asia and the Balkans, the men and women of the U.S. military have performed superbly and sacrificed greatly to protect and advance U.S. national security interests.

In the post-Cold War, post-9/11 era, the United States needs a strong military that is second to none. The U.S. armed forces must be able to conduct a broad range of missions abroad and, as Hurricane Katrina reminded us, here at home. Our armed forces must be able to defend the U.S. homeland; deter and, if necessary, defeat aggression against U.S. allies and interests around the world; help to establish and maintain stability in key regions; destroy terrorist organizations, deny them safe haven, and fight insurgencies; counter the proliferation of weapons of mass destruction to both state and non-state actors; work with the militaries of other countries, and with multilateral and international organizations, to build their capacities for these missions; and help respond to disasters, both manmade and natural, here at home.

Fielding such a military depends in large part on our nation's ability to attract the best and brightest Americans to military service. Since the mid-1980s, the U.S. military has been able to recruit and retain a professional force of high quality volunteers. Indeed, the quality of the people in the force – both active duty and reserve – has been the foundation on which the United States has been able to build the best military in the world.

But this foundation is now being shaken, and America's military is at risk. While the U.S. military has performed superbly in Afghanistan, Iraq, and elsewhere, our ground forces are under enormous strain. This strain, if not soon relieved, will have highly corrosive and potentially long-term effects on the force.[1]

We believe that the Bush administration has broken faith with the American soldier and Marine:
- by failing to plan adequately for post-conflict operations in Iraq;
- by failing to send enough forces to accomplish the mission at an acceptable level of risk; and
- by failing to adequately equip and protect the young Americans they sent into harm's way.

---

[1] Some attribute this strain to the drawdown of U.S. military forces that occurred after the end of the Cold War. Overall, the number of divisions in the active duty Army has gone from 18 at the end of the Cold War to 10 today. Between 1988 and 1992, the first Bush administration reduced the active duty Army by 27% from 781,000 to 572,000. The Clinton administration reduced Army end strength by another 16% to 482,000 – a level endorsed by the George W. Bush administration in its 2001 Quadrennial Defense Review.

These failures have created a real risk of breaking parts of the force – a force that is critical to protecting and advancing our national interests, now and in the future. The American military deserves better. The American people deserve better.

This paper is intended to sound a warning – to raise awareness about the state of our ground forces today and the very real risk that poses to our future security.[2] Breaking our ground forces would put this nation's security in grave danger. We cannot allow this to happen. Therefore, this paper proposes an action plan for restoring the health and vitality of the U.S. military. The administration has under discussion some of what is recommended here, but the actions actually being taken fall far short of what is required.

Right now, in Afghanistan, Iraq, and around the globe, the U.S. military is fighting for us. Today, we are standing up to fight for them.

The Facts

- **Nearly all of the available combat units in the U.S. Army, Army National Guard and Marine Corps have been used in current operations.**

Every available combat brigade from the active duty Army has already been to Afghanistan or Iraq at least once for a 12 month tour.[3] Many are now in their second tours of duty, having had barely a year at home.[4] Some are already slated to go back for a third rotation. In addition, selected high demand units are getting ready to deploy to Iraq for a fourth tour.[5]

In the reserve component, more than 95% of the Army National Guard's combat battalions and all but one of its 10 special operations units have been mobilized since 9/11. This includes units that have been deployed to Operation Enduring Freedom or Operation Iraqi Freedom as well as units supporting operations in the Balkans. Short of full mobilization, there is little or no combat capacity remaining in the Army National Guard that could be available for deployment, without the President declaring a new emergency, given the statutory constraint that individuals cannot be mobilized for more than 24 consecutive months.[6] At the same time, the average length of tour for reservists

---

[2] Although this paper details some of the impacts of current U.S. force deployments, it does not take on the larger question of future U.S. strategy and force posture in Iraq. That critical topic is simply beyond the scope of this paper.

[3] This includes 32 of the Army's original 33 brigade combat teams; the exception is one brigade in Korea. In addition, 9 of the 10 new brigade combat teams being built as part of the Army's transformation to 43 modular brigade combat teams are now deployed or scheduled for deployment.

[4] Two brigades from the10[th] Mountain division are on their second tour in Afghanistan; the Army division and brigades that led the initial assault in 2003 are now returning to Iraq – i.e., units from the 3rd Infantry, 4th Infantry, and 101st Air Assault divisions.

[5] The National Guard Bureau bases this calculation on 60% or more of a unit's members having been mobilized for 18 or more consecutive months.

[6] Under Partial Mobilization Authority (Title 10 of the U.S. Code 12302), following a declaration of a national emergency by the President or the Congress, the President may authorize the service secretaries to order units and individuals (not to exceed 1,000,000) on to active duty for not more than 24 consecutive months. This authority, invoked when President Bush declared a national emergency after 9/11, has been

has more than doubled, from 156 days in Desert Shield/Desert Storm to 342 days in OEIF/OIF.

In addition, 60% of the Army Reserve, comprised primarily of support units, has been mobilized since 9/11. Only 16% of the Army Reserve remains eligible for mobilization to support operations in Iraq and Afghanistan under current authorities, but many of the remaining specialties are not in demand. Fielding the necessary combat support/combat service support units has proven particularly challenging for the Army. In the current rotation in Iraq, 20% of these units are being manned with soldiers that were removed from their original occupational specialties and rapidly retrained to fill empty billets in cobbled-together units.

The Marine Corps is also under tremendous strain. All active duty Marine Corps units are being used on a "tight" rotation schedule of seven months deployed, less than a year home to reset, and then another seven months deployed – meaning that active duty Marine Expeditionary Units (MEUs) are experiencing two operational deployments per cycle rather than the usual one per cycle. In addition, all of the Marine Corps Reserve's combat units have been mobilized.

- **The Army may be experiencing the beginnings of a recruiting crisis.**

The active duty Army began missing its recruiting goals in February 2005, when it fell short of its monthly goal (by 27%) for the first time since 2000. At the end of FY2005, the Army fell 6,627 recruits short of its annual goal of 80,000 new accessions for the active duty force.[7] Although this shortfall is not alarming in and of itself, many expect the recruiting shortfall to be far larger this year if public support for the war in Iraq continues to decline, the demographic of young Americans eligible to serve continues to shrink,[8] the economy continues to offer more attractive alternatives to young job seekers, and the propensity of young Americans to enlist continues to decrease. In addition, some worry that the Army is lowering its quality standards: in October 2005, for example, 19% of Army recruits were drawn from "Category IV" (the lowest aptitude level accepted) – a percentage far higher than the historical average. The coming year will be critical in determining whether the active Army is simply going through a bad patch or entering one of the worst recruiting crises in its history.

---

used to support OEF and OIF. Under Partial Selected Reserve Call-up Authority (10 USC 12304), anytime the President determines that there are insufficient people in the Active forces, he may call units and individuals (not to exceed 200,000) to active duty for not more than 270 days. PSRC was used in the first Gulf War and since then has been used primarily to support peace operations like the Balkans. Governors also have called Guard members to state active duty funded under Title 32 to support homeland security needs. Members of the Guard and Reserves who have already been mobilized for lengthy tours can, however, volunteer for additional deployments.

[7] The goal of recruiting 80,000 troops a year in FY2005-2007 means that the Army must recruit an additional 10,000 troops per year (compared to FY2004). This 30,000 increase in active duty Army end strength over the next three years was requested as a temporary measure to facilitate the Army's transition to a modular force of 43-48 modular brigade combat teams.

[8] The Army estimates that 73% of American youth are not eligible for military service because they do not meet the military's health, education, moral and other standards.

The Army Reserve fell about 16% behind its recruiting target for the year, and the Guard about 20% short of its annual goal. Of particular concern is the downward trend in Army Reserve end strength for FY2005-06. Current authorized and budgeted end strength is 205K, but actual end strength is only about 190K. The Army Reserve now projects increased losses of personnel, which will make achieving its FY2006 end strength target extremely difficult. Although Army National Guard end strength is now 10K short of its authorized level of 350K, in the past few months increased recruiting and retention efforts have begun to narrow this gap.

Part of the problem here is that people leaving the active duty military are no longer signing up for the Guard and Reserves in the numbers that they have in the past. Some are being prevented from leaving the active Army by "stop loss" orders. Others are choosing to stay in the active force. Still others, once they get out, do not want to risk being deployed again as a reservist. As a result, the Army Guard and Reserves have fewer "prior service" personnel and are now in direct competition with the active Army for new recruits.

- **The Army and Marine Corps are meeting their overall retention and attrition goals, for the moment, but some fear that a retention crisis may be looming for the Army.**

The good news is that the Army, Army National Guard and Marine Corps are still meeting their overall retention/attrition targets, thanks in large part to the willingness of young patriots to endure additional danger, hardship and time away from home when their country calls. However, the administration's use of "stop loss" orders to keep members in service beyond their original commitment has skewed the data on retention somewhat and effectively hidden growing personnel deficits, particularly in the Army.[9]

So has the practice of amalgamating retention rates for different parts of the force into a single figure. For example, while the Army Reserve and Army National Guard exceeded their retention goals for careerists, they fell substantially short of their goals for those deciding whether to renew their commitment for the first time, creating the potential for long-term imbalances in the force.

In addition, we are having trouble keeping some of our most highly skilled people in the force. The Bush administration's decision to use large numbers of private contractors on the battlefield in Iraq has had the perverse effect of incentivizing highly trained Special Operations Forces personnel to leave the armed forces in order to work as contractors for much higher pay.

Unfortunately, other indicators suggest a major retention crisis may be on the horizon. Between 2001 and 2004, divorce rates among active duty Army officers tripled, and rates among Army enlisted soldiers grew by 50% as deployments lengthened and

---

[9] Some 9,800 soldiers are currently under "stop loss" orders, and the Army will likely continue stop loss for 7-9,000 soldiers through the end of FY2006 in an effort to maintain the integrity of deployed units.

increased in frequency. Although these divorce rates have begun to decline in the past year, they underscore the severity of the strains on active duty personnel and their families. Similarly, the incidence of domestic violence increased over the same period. These and other warning signs have caused some commanders to fear that personnel who were willing to undertake successive deployments as part of a "surge" may not be willing to sustain this tempo of operations over the long term due to the adverse impacts on their families.

- **The Army and the Army National Guard have experienced critical equipment shortfalls that increased the level of risk to forces deployed in Iraq and Afghanistan and reduced the readiness of units in the United States.**

From the beginning of the Iraq war until as late as last year, the active Army experienced shortages of key equipment items – such as radios, up-armored HMMWVs, trucks, machine guns, rifles, grenade launchers, and night vision equipment – for troops deploying overseas. While many of these shortfalls have now been addressed for deployed units, the readiness ratings of many non-deployed units – based on their manning, equipment, and training levels – have dropped to very low levels (C-3 or C-4).[10] This is particularly worrisome in light of the fact that some of these units are slated to deploy later this year. This situation is even worse for Army National Guard units, many of whom have had to leave their equipment sets in Iraq for arriving units to fall in on. These readiness shortfalls are only likely to grow as the war in Iraq continues to accelerate the wearout rate of all categories of equipment for the ground forces.

The Risks

- **The Army and the Marine Corps cannot sustain today's operational tempo indefinitely without doing damage to their forces.**

Today's tempo of operations is well above what the Army believes it can manage over the long term. Army personnel management policies generally aim for at least two years at home between deployments for active duty personnel and mobilization no more than once every five to six years for Guard and reserve personnel. This is the tempo that the Army believes it can sustain for long periods of time without losing personnel. But the Army cannot sustain its current deployment levels beyond 2006 without either sending active duty forces back to Iraq with less than two years' rest, re-mobilizing reservists, or building additional new brigades. At the moment, none of these options appears viable. Similarly, the Marine Corps can temporarily surge to two deployments per three-year rotation cycle, but it cannot sustain this tempo indefinitely. When personnel are deployed for long tours with great frequency, it becomes exceedingly difficult to recruit high quality volunteers into the force and to keep the best quality personnel from leaving the force.

---

[10] It should be noted that Republicans lawmakers, who during the Clinton administration were quick to demand and hold hearings on the readiness of the armed forces every time a unit went to C-3 or C-4, have essentially looked the other way on force readiness issues during the Iraq war.

- **If recruiting trends do not improve over the next year, the Army – both active and reserve – will experience great difficulty fully manning its planned force structure and providing the needed rotation base for operations in Iraq and Afghanistan.**

A year from now, the combination of fewer than needed recruits and fewer than needed reenlistments in the junior grades could result in a significant "hollowing" and imbalance in the Army, both active and reserve. Based on DoD's monthly manpower report by grade, the Army already has a deficit of some 18,000 personnel in its junior enlisted grades (E1-E4). Even if it meets its recruiting and retention goals, the Army is projected to be short some 30,000 soldiers (not including stop loss) by the end of FY2006.[11] Such a shortfall would force the Army to cannibalize some units in order to fully man others to deploy. This would negatively impact not only the cohesion of the units deploying but also the readiness and usability of those left at home. It would also exacerbate strains on personnel pulled from recently returned units and reassigned to fill out deploying ones. Such manpower shortfalls will also jeopardize aspects of the Army's plan to transform its division-based structure into modular brigade combat teams – the Army may simply not have enough people to populate its planned force structure. These factors will create tremendous internal pressures to redeploy additional U.S. forces from Iraq by next spring, whatever the conditions on the ground may be.

- **If retention rates decline significantly, the viability of the All Volunteer force could be threatened.**

Many observers of the Army and Marine Corps are now waiting for the other shoe – the retention shoe – to drop. The All Volunteer Force is now in historically uncharted waters: fighting a protracted conflict with volunteers rather than draftees. What will happen if the current surge for Iraq becomes the steady state and the Army and Marines are not resourced with the people, units and equipment they need for a long-term fight? When will the dedication and sacrifice of our troops run up against the needs of families and communities? Will they vote with their feet? If they do, what will become of the All Volunteer Force? The conventional wisdom is that while most will stay in the force after one or even two tours, after a third year-long deployment in a compressed time period, many will choose to leave the force. Many senior military officers who lived through the Vietnam era and its aftermath believe that if significant numbers of senior non-commissioned officers and field grade commanders begin to leave the force, this could set off a mass exodus and lead to a "hollowing out" of the Army.

- **In the meantime, the United States has only limited ground force capability ready to respond to other contingencies. The absence of a credible strategic reserve in our ground forces increases the risk that potential adversaries will be tempted to challenge the United States.**

---

[11] With stop loss, the end of FY2006 shortfall is projected to be about 20K.

Since the end of World War II, a core element of U.S. strategy has been maintaining a military capable of deterring and, if necessary, defeating aggression in more than one theater at a time. As a global power with global interests, the United States must be able to deal with challenges to its interests in multiple regions of the world simultaneously. Today, however, the United States has only limited ground force capability ready to respond outside the Afghan and Iraqi theaters of operations. If the Army were ordered to send significant forces to another crisis today, its only option would be to deploy units at readiness levels far below what operational plans would require – increasing the risk to the men and women being sent into harm's way and to the success of the mission. As stated rather blandly in one DoD presentation, the Army "continues to accept risk" in its ability to respond to crises on the Korean Peninsula and elsewhere. Although the United States can still deploy air, naval, and other more specialized assets to deter or respond to aggression, the visible overextension of our ground forces has the potential to significantly weaken our ability to deter and respond to some contingencies.

- **Resetting, recapitalizing and modernizing our nation's ground forces will be no small challenge and will require substantial and sustained investment**.

Severe wear and tear on Army and Marine Corps equipment is increasing the costs of "resetting" the force as units return home. Resetting the force involves rehabilitating and repairing equipment returning from the field so that it can once again meet mission performance standards. Given the harsh environments of Iraq and Afghanistan, this is proving more extensive and expensive than in previous operations. Estimates of the costs of rehabilitating Army equipment coming back from operations overseas continue to grow, and are now expected to be some $40 billion over the next four years.

In addition, both the Army and the Marine Corps expect to see increasing costs associated with recapitalizing aging forces and transforming their capabilities for a broader range of 21st century missions.[12] Moreover, as the active Army's force structure expands from 33 brigades to 42 brigade combat teams under its revised modularity plan, its equipment requirements will increase substantially. It will also need substantial funding to modernize its forces with the Army's Future Combat System. Finally, the equipment requirements associated with enabling the Army National Guard and Army Reserve to serve as a truly "operational reserve" – available as a rotation base to support the active Army on a regular basis – are not yet fully understood, but are expected to be quite large. All this adds up to the need for major investments in the recovery and modernization of our nation's ground forces.

The Way Forward

Timely action is required to preserve the All Volunteer Force, help our ground forces recover fully from the strains of current operations, and rebalance and transform our forces to meet the challenges of the 21st century. Obviously, much will depend on the

---

[12] These issues will be discussed in more detail in the NSAG II's next paper on the budget.

size of deployments in Iraq in the next year or two. Those deployments will be influenced by the state of U.S. ground forces, but should be determined largely by the situation on the ground in Iraq. As the United States Congress put it in the 2006 National Defense Authorization Act, 2006 should be "a period of significant transition to full Iraqi sovereignty, with Iraqi security forces taking the lead for the security of a free and sovereign Iraq, thereby creating the conditions for the phased redeployment of United States forces from Iraq," and "United States military forces should not stay in Iraq any longer than required."[13]

In the meantime, DoD should make maximum use of other strategies to reduce the demands on U.S. ground forces. For example, support units from the Air Force and Navy, which are not overextended, should be substituted for strained Army units to the greatest extent possible. In the current OIF rotation, about 9% of the combat support/combat service support units are being manned by personnel from other services. This practice should be expanded to the greatest extent possible in the coming months.

In addition, the Bush administration should pursue a serious effort to rebuild consensus among allies and partners on a way ahead that leads to greater burden sharing and increased troop contributions from allies and partners. While this may be very difficult in Iraq, increased allied contributions to operations in Afghanistan could nevertheless help reduce the strains on U.S. ground forces overall.

Finally, the administration should do everything in its power to enhance and accelerate the equipping and training of indigenous Iraqi and Afghan security forces. Several years into these supposedly high priority training efforts, there are still reports of indigenous forces lacking basic military equipment, adequate training facilities and essential operating infrastructure. There is simply no excuse for these shortfalls given the importance of the training mission to the success of these operations and ultimately to our ability to bring American troops home.

As our forces draw down in Iraq, the nation must pursue five courses of action to prepare for future military requirements:

1. Fully fund the recovery and transformation of our nation's ground forces.
2. Adapt the roles, missions, organization, training and equipment of the National Guard and Reserves for the future.
3. Increase the deployable capacity of the Army over time by at least 30,000 personnel.
4. Rebalance the mix of capabilities within the U.S. military for 21st century missions.

---

[13] See Section 1227 of the Conference Report of the Fiscal Year 2006 National Defense Authorization Act. This section also requires the President to report to Congress on a number of factors, including the conditions that must be met to transition additional security responsibility to Iraqi security forces, the criteria used to evaluate progress toward meeting such conditions, a plan for meeting such conditions and an assessment of the extent to which they have been met. Iraq is indeed a critical issue, but a more fulsome treatment of Iraq strategy is beyond the scope of this paper.

5. Enhance support for recruiting and retention efforts.

1. Fully fund the recovery and transformation of our nation's ground forces.

In order to restore the health of U.S. ground forces in the wake of Iraq, the nation must step up and invest substantial resources to reset, recapitalize, and modernize the force. Resetting the force is already well underway in both the Army and the Marine Corps and has been funded through emergency supplemental appropriations. The problem is that anticipated equipment rehabilitation costs may well extend beyond the supplemental appropriations for Iraq and Afghanistan, which could leave both the Army and the Marine Corps with substantial unpaid bills. Congress must ensure that even when supplemental funding ends, adequate funding for resetting the force continues. Without this, neither service will be able to "get well" in the wake of Iraq.

At the same time, both the Army and the Marine Corps have a number of systems that are nearing the end of their projected service lives. Both, for example, are faced with the prospect of block obsolescence for whole classes of vehicles. Within the next couple of years, the Army and the Marine Corps will need to embark on major recapitalization programs to keep their forces supplied with reliable, functioning equipment. This will be particularly challenging for the Army as it transitions to a force of more numerous modular brigade combat teams.

In addition, both the Army and the Marine Corps have ambitious plans to modernize and transform their forces to be more capable of executing 21st century missions, and in both cases these plans are vulnerable to cost growth and to being under-funded over time. Restoring the health of both services is not a matter of simply returning them to their status quo ante; it is a matter of ensuring that they are organized, trained, equipped and resourced to meet the full range of traditional and non-traditional challenges in the future.

2. Adapt the roles, missions, organization, training and equipment of the National Guard and Reserves for the future.

Since the end of the Cold War, the National Guard and Reserves have gradually evolved from being a strategic reserve – forces to be mobilized for a major war or national emergency – to an operational reserve – forces that regularly support and provide a rotation base for the operations of the active duty military at home and abroad. This is especially true since 9/11.

The reality is that the operational reserve model is here to stay. Demand for U.S. military forces is likely to remain high (even if not as high as today) and budget, demographic and recruiting realities will preclude a major expansion of the active duty military in the near term. But this new reality is not yet reflected in how reserve forces are being organized, trained, equipped, and funded. Consequently, we have a legacy force making heroic efforts to perform a new set of missions at an unsustainable tempo of operations and without the necessary resources, training and equipment.

The challenge is to figure out how to make the operational reserve model work. The Army National Guard and Army Reserve have proposed putting their forces on a rotation-based footing which would ensure that units would deploy no more than once every five or six years. This new paradigm will require additional investment in equipment and training commensurate with the increased levels of readiness required. It will also require a greater depth of support capabilities within the Guard, both to support the new modular brigades and to enhance the Guard's capacities for civil support missions, like the response to Hurricane Katrina. Perhaps most importantly, it may also require developing a new social compact between the U.S. government and our "citizen soldiers" that clarifies both the new expectations of a more operational reserve and the government's obligations to those who are serving under this new construct.[14]

Given that future demand is likely to span a broad range of missions – from high-intensity combat operations and stability and reconstruction operations to counterterrorism and homeland defense – we need to prepare and resource reserve forces that are capable of conducting a wide variety of operations. In particular, homeland defense is becoming an increasingly important mission for the National Guard, and that should be reflected in how some units of the Guard are equipped and trained.

Given its history, deep ties to local communities and geographic dispersal across the United States, the National Guard remains the force of choice to undertake critical homeland defense missions and to provide military support to civil authorities. The National Guard is ideally suited for steady state missions at home like air defense as well as domestic crisis response missions like consequence management and WMD incident response. The Department of Defense needs to better define the roles and missions of the National Guard in homeland defense and civil support, and the Guard needs to conduct an in-depth assessment of how its organization, training, equipment and force management approaches need to change to meet the associated requirements. Particular attention should be paid to enhancing the National Guard's training and equipment for conducting civil support and consequence management missions.

Both the National Guard and the Reserves also have key roles to play in supporting U.S. military operations overseas, be it providing key capabilities or serving as a rotation base for long-lasting missions. This is particularly true for stabilization and reconstruction operations, where their civilian skills may be of great value. The reserves continue to offer a cost-effective way to rapidly expand the pool of available military forces in crisis or war, and sustain critical links between the U.S. military and the American people.

To date, however, the National Guard and Reserves have not been adequately prepared or resourced for these indispensable roles. This nation needs to invest more in the readiness of the Army Reserve and National Guard. The costs of doing so have been

---

[14] The nature of this new social compact and its implications for the force management, compensation, benefits, etc. of those who serve in a more operational reserve is being explored in a CSIS study forthcoming in June 2006.

estimated to be about $20 billion each for the Army National Guard and the Army Reserve. We also need to explore diversifying the contracts available to reservists to ensure that the U.S. military – and the U.S. government more broadly – can gain greater access to civilians with critical skills (e.g. information technology specialists, linguists, etc.) and that more Americans can serve their country in some capacity.

3. Increase the pool of deployable forces in the Army over time by at least 30,000 personnel.

Looking to the future, the demand for U.S. ground forces is unlikely to remain as high as it is today, but it is likely to remain higher than pre-9/11 levels given the range of security challenges we now face. The struggle against the threat from violent extremists will likely last for years, if not decades. Although this will require the integrated use of all instruments of U.S. national power, fighting terrorists abroad and protecting Americans at home will remain enduring missions for the U.S. military. Given that there is now a clear connection between failed or failing states and terrorists with global reach, the U.S. military will also be called on to conduct operations to deny terrorists safe haven and prevent ungoverned spaces from emerging. This will likely involve greater U.S. military assistance to build the capacity of other militaries and perhaps counterinsurgency operations to shore up friendly but weak governments. The U.S. military will also be tasked with combating the proliferation of weapons of mass destruction in various ways, be it preventing an adversary from using them or securing and eliminating dangerous weapons and materials in the wake of conflict or chaos. In addition, the United States will continue to face potential conflicts with rogue states hostile to U.S. interests and with states who may threaten our allies. And, as we have learned the hard way in Iraq and Afghanistan, if such a war involves regime change, it will require extensive post-conflict stabilization and reconstruction operations, likely of many years duration. Finally, the catastrophic devastation on the Gulf Coast reminds us of the critical roles the military has to play in responding to disasters here at home.

This argues for making permanent the 30,000 person increase in active duty Army end strength that the Congress has authorized but that the Secretary of Defense views as only a temporary measure to facilitate the Army's transition to a more modular force. Making this increase permanent would enable the Army to grow its active duty force structure to at least 48 brigade combat teams (rather than just 42) over time. Such an increase would reduce future strains on the Army given the projected range of future demand.

While increasing the size of the Army would make it easier to meet future operational requirements, it will certainly not be easy. In the near term, recruiting additional soldiers will be difficult, if not impossible – at least until we turn the corner in Iraq. Building additional force structure will take time, both to establish new units and to populate them with trained personnel. Increasing force structure will also be expensive about $1.5 billion for each new brigade plus recurring personnel costs.

Nevertheless, we believe that permanently increasing the active duty Army by at least 30,000 personnel should be pursued as a mid-term goal. Whether the active Army should be increased beyond this level will depend on a whole host of currently unknowable factors: the post-Iraq level of demand for U.S. forces, the extent to which efforts to rebalance the force are effective, the readiness and availability of Guard and reserve forces, recruiting trends post-Iraq, and whether the spiraling costs associated with military personnel can be brought under control.

4. Rebalance the mix of capabilities within the U.S. military for 21st century missions.

Throughout the post-Cold War period, and increasingly since 9/11, the U.S. military has experienced a mismatch between the capabilities it inherited from the Cold War and the capabilities it needs to deal with emerging threats. Forces optimized to fight major conventional wars are now being asked to combat terrorism, conduct stability and reconstruction operations, fight counterinsurgency campaigns, and so on. The mix of capabilities resident in the force needs to be fundamentally rebalanced. We need to ensure that the U.S. military has what it needs not only to fight and win major conventional wars but also to succeed across the full spectrum of operations. This will require four parallel efforts:

- First, the U.S. military must convert units that are in low demand in the new security environment into unit types that are in high demand in order to reduce the most acute strains on the force. The Army is already planning to convert up to 100,000 personnel billets from low demand specialties like air defense and field artillery to high demand specialties like military police and civil affairs. Such conversions should be accelerated and their scope expanded as far as necessary.

- Second, we need to rebalance the mix of capabilities in the active and reserve components and create more stable and predictable schedules for deployment. Currently, there are a number of "high demand/low density" units in the reserve component that are being used almost as frequently as their active duty counterparts. More of these types of units need to be created in the active duty military.[15] In addition, there are some types of forces that are almost always needed in the first 30 days of the military's response to a crisis, yet many currently reside in the reserve component where they are more difficult to access in a timely manner. Secretary Rumsfeld is seeking to move these capabilities into the active force. This makes sense, but only to a point. It is imperative that our armed forces remain structured so as to preserve the essential link between the military and the body politic – to ensure that any President must mobilize substantial numbers of America's "citizen soldiers" in order to go to war. Maintaining this link – and the accountability it brings – was the original intent of the Abrams Doctrine in creating the All Volunteer Force, and it should remain a fundamental design principle of the U.S. armed forces. What is most

---

[15] In a few exceptional cases, such as civil affairs battalions, there may be real limits on how far such rebalancing can be taken, as the skill sets required are more readily found in the civilian workforce than they are cultivated in a professional military context.

needed is a system of preparing, deploying, and resetting these forces that improves their availability to the nation while also enhancing predictability and stability for soldiers and their families.

- Third, we need to take maximum advantage of technology and services offered by the private sector to make the best use of our military personnel. In today's military, there are a number of opportunities where incorporating the latest information technology and "working smarter" could substantially reduce manpower requirements. This is particularly true in the logistics and support arena where many tasks are still done "the old fashioned way." In addition, because military personnel are becoming a scarce commodity and because, over their careers, they are more than twice as expensive as their civilian counterparts,[16] we cannot afford to have military personnel performing jobs that could be performed just as well by civilians. Each of the military services needs to review each military occupational specialty, particularly back office functions like finance and accounting, and ask whether these tasks could be performed in a more cost-effective manner by civilians, either U.S. government employees or contract personnel. Although a good deal of military-civilian conversion and "outsourcing" has already occurred, it has been pursued in a fairly ad hoc manner, sometimes with unintended consequences. DoD needs to rethink how it is using contractors on the battlefield, especially when civilian security forces bleed off skilled U.S. military personnel, while also being more creative about outsourcing non-battlefield tasks that do not have to be performed by someone in uniform

- More broadly, the U.S. government needs to build deployable operational capacity in key civilian agencies like the State Department to conduct critical tasks for which the U.S. military does not have a comparative advantage. Such capacity should include a substantial cadre of full-time professionals who are deployable on a non-volunteer basis for rotations of at least a year, as well as a reserve of on-call experts from outside the U.S. government and substantial contracting authorities to access private sector capabilities. The U.S. also needs to encourage the development of greater international capacity to conduct complex missions like stabilization and reconstruction. In the absence of capable civilian partners in the field, the military is doomed to experience mission creep and no viable exit strategy, and the nation will be saddled with much higher risks and costs.

5. Increase support for recruiting and retention efforts.

Although President Bush has sent the U.S. military to war in Iraq and to fight terrorism around the globe, he has failed to mobilize the American people for either cause. There has been no John F. Kennedy-like "ask not what your country can do for you, but what you can do for your country" speech – no call to national service. This failure of leadership has only widened the gap between the U.S. service personnel and the

---

[16] See GAO Report 05-798 available at http://www.gao.gov/new.items/d05798.pdf.

American people they are risking their lives to protect. It has also left the military services bereft of the most important thing they need to be successful in recruiting young Amcricans to service and retaining those who have made an initial commitment to serve: civilian leadership with a compelling vision and strategy. This country needs a Commander in Chief who can use the U.S. military wisely and inspire a nation of young people to serve. America needs a President who, at a time of national need, will make a serious and sustained effort to call America's young people to serve their country, be it in the military or in some other form of national service.

In the meantime, Congress should continue to give the military services the flexibility they need to tailor and target recruiting and retention incentives to be as effective as possible. In recent years, Congress has acted to increase the bonuses and benefits that can be offered for both recruitment and retention. The 2006 National Defense Authorization Act includes an even wider variety of incentives, from higher cash bonuses to education benefits to down payment assistance for first homes to referral bonuses for serving soldiers who bring in new recruits.

Additionally, we need to think more creatively about diversifying the range of contracts we offer to young Americans who are interested in serving their country. For starters, we need to make it easier for people to transition back and forth between active duty service and the Guard or reserves. We also need to make it easier for people who leave the military to come back into service and for "middle aged" Americans (30- and 40-somethings) to join the military if they meet all the necessary standards. The idea of making a life-long commitment to one organization is an anathema to today's generation of young people. In order to make military service more attractive to them, we need to enhance the variety of experiences and opportunities it can offer them.

We also note with concern the rift that has developed between many of our nation's most elite universities and the U.S. military. In the Vietnam era, many campuses closed their doors to ROTC programs and military recruiters. Given the needs of the nation at this time in our history and the importance of having a military that reflects all sectors of American society, this rift should be healed.

Finally, it would be a mistake to think that a draft can solve our personnel problems and provide the quality soldiers we need. However, we need to broaden our notion of national service beyond military service to take better advantage of two of our nation's greatest strengths – cultural diversity and technological prowess. We need to find ways to bring Americans with critical skill sets, from language skills to computer skills, into national service of some kind, on a full or part time basis.

Conclusion

The strains on the nation's ground forces are serious and growing, and the viability of the All Volunteer Force is at risk. The United States cannot afford to let this to happen. Not only would it be costly, difficult and time-consuming to rebuild a broken force, but allowing the force to break would also endanger U.S. national security. As a global power with global interests, as a nation locked in a long struggle with violent extremists, and as a world leader, the United States cannot allow its military to be weakened any further. We must keep faith with the men and women in our military and with the American people. We need to act now to protect and restore our armed forces.[17]

---

[17] The NSAG would like to thank a number of individuals who made invaluable contributions to this paper, including: David Morrison, David McGinnis, and Shawn Brimley.

Real Security:
Protecting America and Restoring Our Leadership in the World

21st Century Military: Additional Resources

Beyond Goldwater-Nichols Reports (Phase I and Phase II), **Center for Strategic and International Studies.** These reports identify key issues for defense reform. [Available at http://www.csis.org/isp/bgn/reports.htm.]

Restoring American Military Power: A Progressive Quadrennial Defense Review, **Center for American Progress, January 2006.** This report offers an alternative vision of the Quadrennial Defense Review. [Available at: www.americanprogress.org]

The Thin Green Line, **reports by Andrew Krepinevich, Center for Strategic and Budgetary Assessments, 8/04.** These reports discuss the strain on the military due to deployments in Iraq and Afghanistan. [Available at: www.csba.org]

Army Forces for Sustained Operations, **RAND Corporation, 2005.** "This report describes the effects of large deployments on the Army's ability to sustain overseas operations, to provide forces for other contingencies, to ensure that soldiers are trained, and to continue to recruit and retain soldiers." [Available at: www.rand.org]

DOD Needs Action Plan to Address Enlisted Personnel Recruitment and Retention Challenges, **Government Accountability Office, 11/17/05.** This report found that the U.S. military had failed to fully staff 41 percent of its array of combat and noncombat specialties. Specifically, the Army, National Guard and Marines signed up as few as a third of the Special Forces soldiers, intelligence specialists and translators that they had aimed for over the last year. [Available at: http://www.gao.gov/new.items/d06134.pdf]

Improving Post-Conflict Capabilities, **Council on Foreign Relations, September 2005.** The report notes that "argues that the United States must acknowledge that "war-fighting has two important dimensions: winning the war and winning the peace." [Available at: http://www.cfr.org/]

These articles look at private military contractors in Iraq:
> ➤ **"Outsourcing War," by P.W. Singer,** *Foreign Affairs,* **March/April 2005.**
> ➤ **"The Other Army,"** *New York Times,* **8/14/05.**

"Veterans Report Mental Health Distress," *Washington Post, 3/1/06*. Details a U.S. Army study which found that more than one third of soldiers returning from Iraq have sought help for mental health problems. [Available at: http://www.washingtonpost.com/wp-dyn/content/article/2006/02/28/AR2006022801712.html]

The Independent Budget 2006. Examines critical veterans budget issues. [Available at: http://www.pva.org/independentbudget/]

TOTAL NUMBER OF VETERANS, BY STATE

STATE	VETERANS, as of September 2004
Alabama	426,322
Alaska	67,299
Arizona	555,223
Arkansas	268,353
California	2,310,968
Colorado	427,956
Connecticut	268,975
Delaware	80,751
DC	37,377
Florida	1,788,496
Georgia	760,323
Hawaii	107,310
Idaho	133,183
Illinois	896,640
Indiana	550,871
Iowa	265,960
Kansas	246,359
Kentucky	359,845
Louisiana	366,957
Maine	143,726
Maryland	486,298
Massachusetts	490,882
Michigan	836,950
Minnesota	426,591
Mississippi	240,109
Missouri	554,531
Montana	102,605
Nebraska	159,487
Nevada	243,716
New Hampshire	131,074
New Jersey	582,917
New Mexico	180,172
New York	1,171,900
North Carolina	767,051
North Dakota	55,374
Ohio	1,051,683
Oklahoma	355,312
Oregon	366,780
Pennsylvania	1,145,919
Rhode Island	91,161
South Carolina	413,551
South Dakota	73,400
Tennessee	540,778
Texas	1,681,748
Utah	151,129
Vermont	57,802
Virginia	750,950
Washington	632,929
West Virginia	188,101
Wisconsin	474,594
Wyoming	54,941
TOTAL	*24,523,329**

SOURCE: Department of Veterans Affairs, September 2005
*Does not include veterans living in Puerto Rico or other areas.

NUMBER OF VETERANS DENIED HEALTH CARE COVERAGE BECAUSE OF BUSH POLICIES, BY STATE

STATE	VETERANS DENIED VA HEALTH CARE
Alabama	5,004
Alaska	578
Arizona	5,835
Arkansas	4,983
California	17,378
Colorado	3,599
Connecticut	2,651
Delaware	877
DC	164
Florida	27,465
Georgia	7,062
Hawaii	710
Idaho	1,608
Illinois	8,944
Indiana	5,700
Iowa	4,762
Kansas	2,878
Kentucky	4,506
Louisiana	4,893
Maine	2,403
Maryland	3,051
Massachusetts	3,509
Michigan	5,942
Minnesota	5,319
Mississippi	4,308
Missouri	5,552
Montana	1,956
Nebraska	1,991
Nevada	2,111
New Hampshire	1,434
New Jersey	4,808
New Mexico	1,851
New York	9,357
North Carolina	10,405
North Dakota	927
Ohio	9,764
Oklahoma	4,013
Oregon	4,162
Pennsylvania	13,262
Rhode Island	1,045
South Carolina	5,964
South Dakota	1,201
Tennessee	6,165
Texas	19,204
Utah	1,361
Vermont	751
Virginia	5,459
Washington	4,584
West Virginia	2,550
Wisconsin	6,622
Wyoming	777
Total	*261,405*

SOURCE: Department of Veterans Affairs

Real Security:
Protecting America and Restoring Our Leadership in the World

TERRORISM AND WEAPONS OF MASS DESTRUCTION (WMD)

The foremost threat to U.S. national security today comes from violent extremists who are willing to use catastrophic terror, including employing weapons of mass destruction, against innocent Americans in a misguided attempt to advance their cause. Al Qaeda and other like-minded extremist groups aspire to kill large numbers of Americans, disrupt our economy, and impose changes on the international order to accomplish their aims.

To the great detriment of U.S. security, the Bush Administration has failed to grasp the nature of this mounting threat and has proven incapable of advancing a viable strategy to respond to it. Under its misguided policies, Osama bin Laden and key members of Al Qaeda remain at large; extremist groups like Al Qaeda continue to win new converts and are planning to carry out devastating attacks against America and our allies; North Korea and Iran have enhanced their nuclear capabilities; and hundreds of tons of loose nuclear materials remain unsecured and vulnerable to terrorist theft.

Democrats recognize that the most effective means to defeat the threats posed by terrorists and the spread of weapons of mass destruction lies through a comprehensive strategy that employs all aspects of our power – military, intelligence, economic, and diplomatic.

To Defeat Terrorists and Stop the Spread of Weapons of Mass Destruction, Democrats will:

- Eliminate Osama Bin Laden, destroy terrorist networks like al Qaeda, finish the job in Afghanistan and end the threat posed by the Taliban.

- Double the size of our Special Forces, increase our human intelligence capabilities, and ensure our intelligence is free from political pressure.

- Eliminate terrorist breeding grounds by combating the economic, social, and political conditions that allow extremism to thrive; lead international efforts to uphold and defend human rights; and renew longstanding alliances that have advanced our national security objectives.

- Secure by 2010 loose nuclear materials that terrorists could use to build nuclear weapons or "dirty bombs."

- Redouble efforts to stop nuclear weapons development in Iran and North Korea.

Bush/Republican Record on Terrorism/WMD

The Bush Administration's weak strategy in Afghanistan enabled senior al Qaeda leaders to escape and regroup, and its failure to complete the job has left the country vulnerable to drug traffickers and terrorists.

- It is widely believed that many senior Al Qaeda and Taliban officials (including Osama bin Laden) were present in Afghanistan at the start of the conflict and were able to avoid capture because there were insufficient U.S. troops on the ground to cut off escape routes to Pakistan.

- Retired Army Colonel Hy Rothstein's Pentagon-commissioned assessment of the planning and execution of the Afghanistan campaign states that the "failure to adjust U.S. operations in line with the post-Taliban change in theater conditions cost the United States some of the fruits of victory and imposed additional, avoidable humanitarian and stability costs on Afghanistan."

- According to the UN, Afghanistan is again the world's leading opium producer and is in danger of "reverting to a terrorist breeding ground," in light of "troubling indications that remnants of the Taliban and other extremist groups are reorganizing." [*New Yorker*, 4/12/04; UN Reports February 2005 and August 2005]

By opting to pursue a war of choice in Iraq, the Bush Administration diverted scarce resources from the war on terror, which enabled al Qaeda to morph into an expansive movement, fueled other terrorist organizations, and turned Iraq into what it was not before the war – a terrorist training ground and launching pad.

- Special Forces and other military personnel, translators, and critical intelligence assets and personnel were all pulled from Afghanistan in 2002 to prepare for the Iraq war. [Knight-Ridder, 11/26/03]

- According to a May 2004 London-based Institute for Strategic Studies report, "Al-Qaeda's recruitment and fundraising efforts had been given a major boost by the U.S. invasion of Iraq."

- The U.S. invasion of Iraq has advanced al Qaeda's ideological appeal, empowering the group to expand its ranks and improve its capacity to regenerate and launch deadly attacks.

- According to the National Intelligence Council, Iraq has become a terrorist "training ground" and is breeding a new generation of "professionalized" terrorists. [*Washington Post* 1/14/05]

- Terrorism expert Peter Bergen warns that "the current war in Iraq will generate a ferocious blowback of its own, which – as a recent classified CIA assessment predicts – could be longer and more powerful than that from Afghanistan. Foreign volunteers fighting U.S. troops today will find new targets around the world after the war ends." ["Blowback Revisited." *Foreign Affairs*, November 2005.]

Terrorist attacks have dramatically increased on this Administration's watch and its ineffective policies have placed America in a reactive mode.

- According to statistics released by the U.S. Department of State, 2003 saw the highest incidence of terror attacks in over two decades, and then, in 2004, that number tripled. The National Memorial Institute for the Prevention of Terrorism reports that this trend continued in 2005, with attacks up by an additional 51 percent.

- The Administration's one-track policy of "capturing and killing" specific terrorists mistakenly assumes that this policy will end global terrorism. ["Combating Al Qaeda and the Militant Islamic Threat." RAND Corporation, Feb. 2006]

- Without a strategy to understand the enemy – an effective campaign to win hearts and minds in the Muslim world – the U.S. will remain reactive. ["Combating Al Qaeda and the Militant Islamic Threat." RAND Corporation, Feb. 2006]

The Bush Administration launched a war of choice in Iraq largely based on claims about Saddam Hussein's WMD, yet has failed to focus on the gravest WMD threat in the world today – tons of unsecured nuclear material that could make their way into the hands of terrorists.

- There are hundreds of tons of unsecured nuclear material around the world vulnerable to theft, particularly in Russia and former Soviet Union countries. [The Race to Secure Russia's Loose Nukes: Progress Since 9/11." Henry L. Stimson Center and The Center for American Progress, 9/05]

- In February of 2005, CIA Director, Porter Goss declared in testimony before the Senate Intelligence Committee that "there is sufficient material unaccounted for so that it would be possible for those with know-how to construct a nuclear weapon."

- Al Qaeda has made clear its intentions to gain WMD: bin Laden declared it a "religious duty" to obtain nuclear weapons to threaten the U.S. and American interests. [PBS, Frontline Interview 12/23/98]

- In the four years following 9/11, less nuclear material was secured than in the four years prior to the attacks. ["What does the United States Need to Do", Lawrence Korb in *Transforming Homeland Security: US and European Approaches*, Center for Transatlantic Relations, 2006]

- At the current rate, it could take between 12 and 37 years to secure just the weapons-usable nuclear materials located in the countries that make up the former Soviet Union. [The Race to Secure Russia's Loose Nukes: Progress Since 9/11." Henry L. Stimson Center and The Center for American Progress, 9/05]

The Bush Administration has failed to stop, let alone roll back, North Korea's nuclear program.

- On the Bush Administration's watch, North Korea has withdrawn from the Nuclear Non-Proliferation Treaty, kicked out international inspectors monitoring rods containing nuclear material, and quadrupled its nuclear arsenal. Expert estimate North Korea's stockpile has grown from one to two weapons to at least 8 and perhaps as many as 12 weapons.

- The Administration has been unable to develop a coherent policy toward North Korea. As a result, the North Korean threat has grown and America has been made less secure.

The Bush Administration's failure to uphold global nonproliferation treaties has increased the nuclear ambitions of some countries and dramatically raised the specter of nuclear terrorism.

- The threat of terrorists acquiring nuclear weapons or nuclear materials is very real, and increases when countries like Iran and North Korea enhance their nuclear programs.

- North Korea is a brazen proliferator: it is known to sell missiles and nuclear technology and participate in illicit activities, including smuggling, counterfeiting and the drug trade.

- Experts fear that North Korea's severe economic crisis could give way to regime collapse and could set loose its nuclear arsenal.

- The Iranian regime shows little respect for international norms: it has concealed its uranium enrichment activities for nearly two decades, while purporting to seek only a civilian nuclear program and claiming its commitment to nonproliferation as a signatory member of the NPT.

Bush Administration policies that disrespect the rule of law and demonstrate contempt for international standards and institutions have increased the risk to U.S. troops, harmed our efforts to lead an international coalition to fight the war on terror, and weakened our ability to address the next generation of terrorists.

- Abuse of prisoners in Iraq and Afghanistan, secret detentions and renditions, warrantless surveillance in the United States, ignoring the Geneva Conventions, and a go-it-alone foreign policy under the Bush Administration have increased the risks to our troops, effectively alienated key U.S. allies, and been used as recruiting tools for terrorist organizations.

- Recent polls indicate that large majorities of Europeans hold an unfavorable view of America and see the U.S. as posing the greatest threat to international security. ["The Limits of Rice's Diplomacy." Ivo Daaldler, The Brookings Institute, 1/27/06]

Democratic Record on Terrorism/WMD

Comprehensive Strategy to Win the Global War on Terrorism

Democrats Have Called for a Comprehensive Strategy to Win the Global War on Terror. In contrast to the Bush Administration's piecemeal approach, both Senate and House Democrats have advanced a comprehensive U.S. strategy to combat religious extremism and win the war on international terrorism. This strategy calls for increasing special operations forces, curbing terrorist financing, preventing the growth of radical fundamentalism, and advancing U.S. interests through diplomacy and development in the Middle East, Central Asia, South Asia, and Southeast Asia.. [e.g., Biden bill, S. 12, *Targeting Terrorists More Effectively Act of 2005*]

Senate and House Democrats Have Voted for Key Measures to Strengthen the War on Terror. Both Senate and House Democrats have fought for measures to strengthen the war on terror. For example, Senate Democrats supported a Lautenberg amendment that is designed to stop the flow of money to terrorist organizations. The measure would have barred foreign subsidiaries of U.S. companies from doing business with countries considered sponsors of terrorism. Republicans defeated this amendment. [Lautenberg amendment to S. 2845, 2004 Senate Vote #194, 9/30/04, tabled 47-41; Lautenberg amendment to S. 1042; 2005 Senate Vote #203, defeated 47-51] House Democrats voted for a motion to recommit the FY 2005 Intelligence Authorization bill that would have provided for <u>full funding</u> of counter-terrorism programs; Republicans defeated the motion. [2004 House Vote #299, 6/23/04, 197-224] House Democrats have also fought for more funding for language proficiency in the intelligence community, in order to improve our counterterrorism efforts; but Republicans have defeated these efforts. [Reyes amendment to *H.R. 3289, 2003 House Vote #555*, 10/17/03, 206-221]

Keeping WMD Out of the Hands of Terrorists/Securing Loose Nuclear Materials

Senate and House Democrats Have Voted for Greater Efforts to Keep WMD Out of the Hands of Terrorists. Both Senate and House Democrats have been fighting for measures that will strengthen nuclear non-proliferation and programs to secure loose nuclear materials in the former Soviet Union and elsewhere. For example, Senate Democrats supported a Levin amendment to the FY 2005 Defense Authorization bill that would have transferred $515 million from missile defense to nuclear non-proliferation and other anti-terrorism activities. Republicans defeated this important amendment, by a vote of 44 to 56. [2004 Senate Vote #133, 3/22/04]. House Democrats have also fought to increase investments in securing loose nuclear materials. For example, Rep. David Obey (D-WI) sought to offer an amendment to the FY 2003 Iraqi Supplemental that would have provided an additional $2.5 billion for homeland security, including an additional $175 million for nuclear non-proliferation activities. These non-proliferation activities included securing radioactive materials that terrorists can use to construct "dirty bombs." However, Republican blocked the Obey amendment by a vote of 217 to 195. [*2003 House Vote #104*, 4/3/03]

Democrats Have Fought for <u>Strong</u> Intelligence Reform, Implementing the Recommendations of the 9/11 Commission

House and Senate Democrats fought for <u>strong</u> intelligence reform in 2004. In 2004, House and Senate Democrats fought vigorously for the full implementation of the 9/11 Commission's 41 recommendations, issued in July 2004, including the Commission's call for a strong, new Director of National Intelligence. On October 6, 2004, the Senate passed a strong, bipartisan Intelligence Reform bill, by a vote of 96 to 2, that fully carried out the 9/11 Commission's recommendations and received the endorsement of the 9/11 Commissioners and families. However, House Republican leaders favored a weaker bill, with a much weaker Director of National Intelligence. On October 8, House Democrats voted for a motion to recommit that would have replaced the weaker House intelligence reform bill with the strong Senate bill; however, Republicans defeated the motion by a vote of 193 to 223. [*2004 House Vote #522*, 10/8/04] (Ultimately, with Democratic pressure, the conference report was closer to the Senate bill.)

In Order to Improve Intelligence Operations, Democrats Call for Bipartisan Investigation of the Development and Use of Pre-War Intelligence

Democrats Are Calling for a Bipartisan Investigation of Pre-War Intelligence on Iraq WMD. Both Senate and House Democrats have pushed for a bipartisan investigation of the role of policymakers in the development and use of intelligence related to the war in Iraq, particularly pre-war intelligence on the issue of Iraq's WMD. [*2003 Senate Vote #287*, 7/17/03; *2003 Senate Vote #395*, 10/17/03]

Democrats Work to Restore America's Leadership

Democrats Have Worked to Prohibit Torture and Ensure Appropriate Treatment of Detainees. Democrats have advanced efforts to ensure that U.S. treatment of detainees meets the requirements of the Geneva Conventions. [e.g., Biden bill, S. 12, *Targeting Terrorists More Effectively Act of 2005*] In addition, in the Senate, a measure prohibiting the use of torture or cruel and inhumane treatment of detainees and requiring interrogators at military prisons to comply with the Army Field Manuel of Intelligence Interrogation was passed by a strong bipartisan vote of 90 to 9. [2005 Senate Vote #249, 10/5/05] However, it was Democrats who led the effort to pass the same measure in the House, over the opposition of the House Republican Leadership. House Democrats were ultimately successful on December 14, 2005. [*2005 House Vote #630*, 12/14/05]

Democrats Have Fought to Investigate Allegations of Mistreatment of Detainees. Democrats strongly support helping to restore America's leadership in the world by requiring an investigation of U.S. detainee abuses. Democrats believe that establishing an independent, bipartisan investigation of the detainee abuses that have occurred would be enormously beneficial for U.S. relationships abroad and convince the world that these abuses won't happen again. For example, in June 2005, House Democrats supported an amendment to establish an independent, bipartisan commission to investigate U.S. abuses of detainees, but Republicans blocked the amendment by a vote of 197 to 228. [*2005 House Vote #289*, 6/21/05]

Rhetoric vs. Reality on Terrorism/WMD

Rhetoric: "Despite the violence and the suffering the terrorists are wreaking, we're winning the war on terror." [President Bush, Feb 9, 2006 speech]

Reality: Brigadier General Robert L. Caslen, the Pentagon's deputy director for the war on terrorism: "Thirty new terrorist organizations have emerged since the September 11, 2001 attacks, outpacing U.S. efforts to crush the threat." "We are not killing them faster than they are being created." [*Washington Times* 3/2/06; General Caslen, Woodrow Wilson Center speech]

Rhetoric: "The al-Qaeda network has been significantly degraded." [The Administration's National Security Strategy 2006]

Reality: "Al Qaeda terrorism remains the most serious threat to U.S. national security, and the insurgency in Iraq shows no sign of abating, the nation's top intelligence official told the Senate yesterday. … The merger of al Qaeda with the Iraq-based terror group headed by Abu Musab al Zarqawi has extended the reach of the group and broadened its ideological appeal." [*Washington Times* story on the testimony of Director of National Intelligence John Negroponte, 2/3/06]

Rhetoric: "Iraq [is] the central front in the war on terror." [President Bush's UN speech, 9/23/03]

Reality: Iraq was at best on the periphery of the war on terror until the Bush Administration's decision to invade.

- The U.S. Army War College reported that the "Iraq war diverted attention and resources away from the security of the American homeland against further assault by an undeterrable al Qaeda." [BBC, 1/13/04]

- Republican and Democratic experts are increasingly suggesting that the Iraq war has diverted momentum, troops and intelligence resources from the worldwide campaign to destroy the remnants of al Qaeda. [Knight-Ridder, 11/26/03]

- "By invading Iraq, the Bush administration created a self-fulfilling prophecy: Iraq has now replaced Afghanistan as a magnet, a training ground and an operational basis for jihadists, with plenty of American targets to shoot at." [*Christian Science Monitor*, 3/15/06]

Rhetoric: "The Taliban are gone from the scene, the terrorist camps are closed, and our coalition's work there continues, confronting terrorist remnants, training a new Afghan army and providing security as the new government takes shape. Under President Karzai's leadership and with a new constitution, the Afghan people are reclaiming their own country, and building a nation that is secure, independent and free." [Vice President Cheney, 3/17/04]

Rhetoric: "Al-Qaeda has lost its safe haven in Afghanistan." [The Administration's National Security Strategy 2006]

Reality: According to Afghanistan's Defense Minister, ""There has been ... more money and more weapons flowing into [terrorists'] hands in recent months." "We see similarities between the type of attacks here and in Iraq." [AP 11/16/05]

Rhetoric: In October 2001, Bush pledged "to keep the world's most dangerous weapons out of the hands of the world's most dangerous people." [President Bush, 10/01]

Reality: President Bush has underfunded key nonproliferation programs and efforts to secure loose nuclear materials. [*Restoring American Leadership*, John Wolfsthal, Center for American Progress/The Century Foundation, April 2005]

Critics of Bush/Republican Record on Terrorism/WMD

Rand Beers, former Bush Administration National Security Council special assistant and senior director for combating terrorism: "The administration wasn't matching its deeds to its words in the war on terror. They're making us less secure, not more." "The difficult, long-term issues both at home and abroad have been avoided, neglected or shortchanged and generally underfunded."

The bipartisan 9/11 Commission gave the Bush Administration a "D" for its inadequate efforts to prevent terrorists from gaining access to weapons of mass destruction. While "there simply is no higher priority on the national security agenda," it faulted the Administration's lack of leadership and weak initiatives for securing weapons grade nuclear material and preventing terrorists from gaining access to weapons of mass destruction, stating that "current efforts fall far short" of what must be done, given "the potential for catastrophic destruction." [Final Report of the 9/11 Public Discourse Project, December 2005]

Richard Clarke, former Bush Administration National Security Council Official: "Fighting Iraq had little to do with fighting the war on terrorism, until we made it (so)." [Knight Ridder 11/26/03]

Porter Goss, CIA Director: "The Iraq conflict, while not a cause of extremism, has become a cause for extremists." [Testimony before the Senate Intelligence Committee, February 16, 2006.]

Robert Novak, conservative columnist: "The overlooked war [in Afghanistan] continues with no end in sight. Narcotics trafficking is at an all-time high. If U.S. forces were to leave, the Taliban -- or something like it -- would regain power. The U.S. is lost in Afghanistan, bound to this wild country and unable to leave...The situation in Afghanistan, as laid out to me, looks nothing like a country alleged to be progressing toward representative democracy under American tutelage." [*Chicago Sun-Times* 05/31/04]

Afghan Defense Minister Rahim Wardak: Osama bin Laden's al Qaeda network has increased its activities in Afghanistan. "There has been ... more money and more weapons flowing into their hands in recent months." "We see similarities between the type of attacks here and in Iraq." [AP 11/16/05]

Bush Administration incompetence on non-proliferation. Jack Pritchard, former State Department Senior Expert for North Korea and the special envoy for negotiations under the Bush Administration: The "administration's refusal to engage directly with the country made it almost impossible to stop Pyongyang from going ahead with its plans to build, test and deploy nuclear weapons." [*Los Angeles Times*]

Real Security:
Protecting America and Restoring Our Leadership in the World

Summary: *Worst Weapons in Worst Hands: U.S. Inaction on the Nuclear Terror Threat Since 9/11, and a Path of Action.* **The National Security Advisory Group, July 2005.**

This report examines the U.S. government's record in the global war on terror and its efforts counter the threat of weapons of mass destruction (WMD) since September 11, 2001, focusing specifically on the threat of nuclear terrorism. It details the shortcomings of current U.S. strategy to keep the worst weapons – WMD – out of the worst hands – terrorists, arguing that the administration "is fighting a global war on terror, but not yet a global war on WMD." The report describes actions that can be taken to effectively lead such a global war on WMD: to secure all "loose nukes", to strengthen the Non-Proliferation regime and to roll back the nuclear threats of Iran and North Korea.

Summary: *Combating Catastrophic Terror,* **Center for American Progress, October 2005.**

"This paper describes the US need for a long-term strategy to counter the threat of violent Islamic extremism and catastrophic terror. It explains how leading experts and top-ranking officials analyzed the state of US national security preparedness, and concluded that the United States did not feature a counter-terrorism strategy sufficient enough to adequately respond to the threats of violent terrorist groups. The paper presents the suggestions of senior foreign policy experts and their strategic roadmap for successfully meeting the challenges posed by catastrophic terrorism."

Worst Weapons In Worst Hands:

U.S. Inaction On The Nuclear Terror Threat Since 9/11, And A Path Of Action

The National Security Advisory Group
July 2005

William J. Perry, Chair

Madeleine K. Albright, Graham T. Allison, Samuel R. Berger, Ashton B. Carter, Wesley K. Clark, Thomas E. Donilon, Michele A. Flournoy, John D. Podesta, Susan E. Rice, John M. Shalikashvili, Wendy R. Sherman, Elizabeth D. Sherwood-Randall, James B. Steinberg

This study was made possible by the generous philanthropic vision of Walter H. Shorenstein

WORST WEAPONS IN WORST HANDS:
U.S. INACTION ON THE NUCLEAR TERROR THREAT SINCE 9/11, AND A PATH OF ACTION

The National Security Advisory Group
William J. Perry, Chair

THREE YEARS AFTER 9/11, SLEEPWALKING ON WMD

- The gravest threat facing Americans today is a terrorist detonating a nuclear bomb in one of our cities. The National Security Advisory Group (NSAG) judges that the Bush administration is taking <u>insufficient actions</u> to <u>counter this threat.</u>
  - If this catastrophe were to occur, what would we wish we had done to prevent it?
  - <u>Why are those actions not being taken today?</u>

- President Bush has aptly noted that keeping the worst weapons – WMD – out of the hands of the worst people – terrorists – is an American president's highest priority.
  - In the first presidential debate, the moderator asked the two candidates, "What is the single most serious threat to the national security of the U.S.?" Kerry and Bush agreed: nuclear terrorism. As the President said, "I agree with my opponent that <u>the biggest threat facing the country is weapons of mass destruction in the hands of a terrorist network.</u>"
  - In the final weeks of the campaign, Vice President Cheney made nuclear terrorism a centerpiece of his stump speech, arguing that "the biggest threat we face now as a nation is the possibility of terrorists ending up in the middle of one of our cities with deadlier weapons than have ever been used against us... nuclear weapons able to threaten the lives of hundreds of thousands of Americans." According to Cheney, "That's the ultimate threat. For us to have a strategy that's capable of defeating that threat, you've got to get your mind around that concept."

- The NSAG agrees. Yet on the record to date, we judge that <u>the U.S. government has not made the connections between these words and the necessary actions.</u>
- The administration is fighting a global war on terror, but not yet a global war on WMD.
- This NSAG report details the actions that would constitute such a global war on WMD.
- The NSAG's advice is directed to the American public, to the administration, and to members of Congress of both parties.

REPORT CARD ON ACTIONS TO COUNTER WMD AFTER 9/11

Actions taken
- The <u>invasion of Iraq</u> was the principal action taken to counter WMD after 9/11, but, in fact, no WMD were found.
- The <u>renunciation of WMD by Qadaffi's Libya</u> was a major success of U.S. and British cooperative diplomacy extending over two administrations.
- The <u>exposure of the A.Q. Khan network</u> by member states of the Proliferation Security Initiative stopped some trafficking in WMD technology, but an unknown amount is unaccounted for and the black market may still be functioning.

Serious setbacks
- <u>North Korea</u> quadrupled its nuclear arsenal with impunity, and may now be so emboldened by U.S. acquiescence that it cannot be turned back.
- <u>Iran</u> has retained its nuclear program for four years since 9/11, with the U.S. response limited to rhetoric, finally giving belated and tepid support for a European-led initiative. Iranian nuclear ambitions have become more entrenched because of U.S. inaction.

Inaction
- <u>Efforts to secure "loose nukes,"</u> like the Nunn-Lugar program, <u>are little changed</u> from their pre-9/11 levels.
- Diplomatic efforts to <u>strengthen the Nuclear Nonproliferation Treaty</u> were touted by President Bush but have not produced results.

This NSAG memo describes actions that can be taken to expedite the securing of all "loose nukes", to strengthen the NPT system and to reverse the setbacks U.S. nuclear security has already suffered from North Korea and Iran.

NORTH KOREA'S RUNAWAY NUCLEAR PROGRAM: OUT OF CONTROL SINCE 9/11

The Growing Danger to America
- North Korea's runaway nuclear program could be a direct path to nuclear terror:
  - By sale: North Korea sells missiles and other dangerous technology worldwide, with no apparent limits or compunction.
  - By criminal diversion: North Korea's leaders and elite engage in smuggling, counterfeiting, and other illicit activities. These same people might traffic in nuclear materials the way A.Q. Khan trafficked in Pakistan's nuclear technology.
  - By collapse: The North Korean regime could implode if it stays on its current stifling economic path, or suffer a chaotic transition if it undertakes needed reform (like the collapse of the Soviet Union). In either scenario, its nuclear arsenal could "break loose."
- To the risk of terrorism must, of course, be added the obvious danger of nuclear weapons in the hands of the North Korean government itself. Nukes in leader Kim Jong Il's hands:
  - Weaken deterrence on the Korean peninsula, increasing the chance of a horrible war,
  - Risk a domino effect of proliferation in East Asia (Japan, South Korea, Taiwan),
  - And jeopardize the entire global non-proliferation system, unleashing more nuclear programs and thereby more sources of potential nuclear terrorism.
- Apart from these nuclear dangers, failure to stop a development the United States has called "unacceptable" and failure to exert leadership in a group we ourselves have created (China, South Korea, Japan, and Russia in the Six-Party Talks), could cripple the entire U.S. strategic position in East Asia.

The Record since 9/11
- Since 9/11, in the face of North Korea's runaway nuclear program, U.S. policymakers:
  - Did nothing as North Korea crossed redline after redline;
  - Claimed credit for diplomatic process (the Six-Party Talks) but have taken no responsibility for total lack of results;
  - Attempted to outsource the issue to China and then blame the failure on China;
  - Tried to blame the Clinton administration, the administration that actually stopped plutonium production in North Korea.
    - The scorecard
      - Bush I: one to two bombs' worth of plutonium
      - Clinton: zero plutonium
      - Bush II: 4-6 nuclear weapons' worth of plutonium and counting

- The current U.S. administration says it is pursuing a diplomatic path to stop the North Korean nuclear program, but the facts are not consistent with this claim:
  - President Bush has apparently not resolved the bureaucratic dispute between those in his administration who favor diplomacy and those who favor an alternative strategy of pressure or regime change;
  - U.S. negotiators have therefore been sent out with (a) no negotiating position (Assistant Secretary of State Kelly's first three rounds), (b) a bureaucratic compromise position that is vague and indecisive (Kelly's fourth round), (c) a ban on talking directly to the North Koreans;
  - U.S. leaders make statements about North Korean absolute leader Kim Jong Il that seem deliberately intended to undermine the diplomatic path.
- In the absence of a U.S. strategy, American options have narrowed. <u>The U.S. is in a far worse position to stop North Korea diplomatically than it was on 9/11.</u>
  - The plutonium at Yongbyon is out – and the North Koreans say they are making bombs with it;
  - More plutonium is in the making at the Yongbyon reactor;
  - An unchecked uranium enrichment program has had four years to grow;
  - North Korea is boasting of becoming a nuclear power;
  - Except for Japan, the parties the Bush administration brought together to deal with North Korea are all criticizing the U.S. rather than following its leadership.

<u>What Should Be Done Now: An Alternative Diplomatic and Military Strategy</u>
- The Six-Party Talks are set to resume late in July, after being stalled for over a year. During this time North Korea's nuclear program has continued.
- North Korea might still be stopped diplomatically through the Six-Party talks, but to have a chance:
  - President Bush must put an end to the debate within his administration between those who favor diplomacy and those who favor pressure/regime change;
  - Diplomacy or pressure/regime change is not a <u>choice</u>; it is a <u>sequence</u>;
  - The U.S. should devise a <u>Plan A</u> for diplomatic success to employ first, and then a contingent <u>Plan B</u> for pressure to use if diplomacy fails;
  - <u>Plan B</u> serves two purposes: to aid <u>Plan A</u> by showing North Korea the penalty for failing to end its nuclear program; and to create a realistic prospect of containing and ultimately eliminating the nuclear threat from North Korea.
- <u>Plan A</u> should include:
  - A U.S.-crafted position coordinated with China, Russia, and our allies;
  - A results-oriented tempo of diplomacy: frequent meetings (certainly not once per year), at which U.S. negotiators participate actively, and progress or lack of progress is clearly recorded;
  - An objective of total elimination of North Korea's nuclear and missile programs, with fully adequate verification;
  - U.S. willingness to:
    - Pledge not to attack North Korea;
    - Renounce efforts to force a regime change;

Provide Nunn-Lugar-type assistance for dismantlement; and
Progressively deepen diplomatic and economic relations.
- South Korea, China, Japan, and Russia willingness to offer economic and political inducements;
- At this late date in North Korea's nuclear program, it is not clear that North Korea <u>can</u> be persuaded to give up its aspirations for nuclear weapons, so it might be necessary to turn to pressure (Plan B). But the success of Plan B's political and economic dimensions depend on cooperation from China and South Korea, which will not be forthcoming unless they believe that Plan A has been tried and failed; thus a failure to pursue diplomacy via <u>Plan A</u> will make any <u>Plan B</u> ineffective.

- <u>Plan B</u> should combine containment and pressure.
  - Political pressure to deprive the North Korean government of international legitimacy and to undermine it within its borders;
  - Economic pressure via sanctions and embargo, assisted by as many nations as the United States can enlist; and aggressive prosecution of the wide range of illicit activities sponsored by the North Korean government;
  - Military pressure to include the threat of strikes on North Korean WMD production, testing, and deployment facilities;
  - Robust steps to enhance deterrence of attack by North Korea upon any other nation.

Sadly, the developments in North Korea's nuclear weapon program during the U.S. inaction these past few years has made Plan A less likely of success, and Plan B more difficult to implement.

IRAN'S NUCLEAR PROGRAM: MORE ENTRENCHED SINCE 9/11

The Growing Danger to America

- Iran's devious behavior indicates that it is racing to join the nuclear weapons club:
    - Long hidden ambitions: Iran concealed significant enrichment activities for almost two decades although it claims only to want to assure its fuel supply for seven planned civilian nuclear reactors to be built by 2020.
    - Serial confessor: Iran has shamelessly lied about many aspects of its program until confronted with solid evidence to the contrary.
    - #1 state sponsor of terror: Iran has meddled in Iraq and Afghanistan, armed militants hostile to Israel and harbored al Qaeda suspects.
- A nuclear Iran threatens regional and global security by:
    - Escalating fears of vulnerability: Iran's missiles are capable of carrying a nuclear warhead to Israel and Europe and to U.S. forces in Iraq and Afghanistan.
    - Increasing the chance of a domino effect: nuclear aspirants including Egypt, Saudi Arabia, and Syria to acquire nuclear weapons.
    - Endangering world oil supplies.

The Record since 9/11

- Current U.S. government has <u>no viable plan</u> for stopping Iran.
    - President Bush has said a nuclear Iran is unacceptable – but has made no meaningful effort to stop it.
    - Administration <u>infighting</u> has stalled policy formation.
- U.S. <u>subcontracted the problem</u> to the EU3 (France, UK and Germany) but has provided only lukewarm support to them.
    - EU3 obtained Iran's agreement to suspend temporarily its enrichment activities and adhere to the Additional Protocol during negotiations.
    - Following President Bush's first trip to Europe in 2005, the Administration decided to help Europe sweeten the negotiating pot in exchange for European assurances to support sanctions on Iran if negotiations fail.
    - The fragile agreement hangs by a thread: Iranian public opinion strongly favors pursuing nuclear technology; Iranian officials continuously threaten to resume enrichment; and with the recent presidential election, Iran's pro-nuclear conservatives have further consolidated their power.
- The absence of a feasible U.S. policy has left negotiations weak:
    - EU3 lacks complete U.S. backing necessary to compile a deal-making package.
    - U.S. does not want to be seen as bargaining with Iran.
    - Iran has painted itself into a corner with avowals not to step back from its right to enrich, making an agreement with the EU3 or U.S. improbable.
- <u>A nuclear Iran</u> would be a <u>grave failure</u> of this Administration's policy.

What Should Be Done Now: An Alternative Diplomatic and Military Strategy

- To achieve any deal the U.S. government must settle on a course of action.
- A <u>five-year global moratorium</u> on all new enrichment and reprocessing, as called for by Mohammed ElBaradei, is the key.
    - Will require international cooperation in assembling both a bundle of carrots and an arsenal of sticks.
    - U.S., the EU3, Russia, and the IAEA need to present Iran with a bargain, packaged as an offer Iran cannot refuse.
    - It would offer cover for Iran to comply with an international obligation without explicitly yielding to American or EU3 demands.
- <u>The doable deal</u>:
    - EU3 delivery of important economic benefits under the terms of an agreement. Iran is eagerly seeking trade and investment.
    - No U.S. objection to the supply of spare parts for U.S.-origin aircraft and negotiations with Iran about its entrance into the WTO.
    - Credible assurances by the U.S. not to attack Iran to change its regime by force – if Iran ceases all work on its reprocessing and enrichment facilities that could support a nuclear weapons program.
    - Slow-rolling of fuel delivery by Russia until Iran agrees to comply with the five-year moratorium.
    - A combined Russian-EU guarantee to give Iran the opportunity to buy additional civilian nuclear reactors.
    - A promise by Russia to provide an internationally-guaranteed supply of fuel for these reactors and removal of spent fuel at bargain prices.
- <u>Carrots are not enough</u>:
    - Iran should be concerned that it has no realistic possibility of making its enrichment and reprocessing facilities operational.
    - Accordingly, Iran should understand the existential threat of a military response under some conditions.

    If Iran agrees to the moratorium, in an appropriately verifiable way, and we maintain the status quo on all other issues with Iran (i.e., human rights, being the #1 state sponsor of terrorism), we will be no worse off then we were yesterday on other issues in this relationship.

LOOSE NUKES IN RUSSIA AND ELSEWHERE: STILL TOO MANY LOOSE AFTER 9/11

The Danger to America

Paying Russians to take action is no longer effective.

- The logic of prevention needs to be reframed.
    - Putin needs to feel in his gut the <u>existential threat</u> to Moscow of Beslan-caliber terrorists with nuclear weapons.
    - Bush and Putin made some progress on accountability at Bratislava, but more must be done.
- To prevent terrorist nuclear attacks on both New York and Moscow, Russia and the U.S. must jointly:
    - Establish a new <u>"gold standard"</u> by which each nation's methods of securing its own weapons and material are sufficiently transparent to give others confidence that their stockpiles cannot be used by terrorists.
    - <u>Lock down vulnerable weapons and materials</u> worldwide and clean out those facilities that cannot be locked down.
    - Operate with <u>reciprocal transparency</u> so that both governments can assure one another that their weapons and material are being contained and secured.
- Growing extremism in the Caucasus makes nuclear theft in Russia more likely.
    - Chechens have cased Russian nuclear facilities.
- <u>The top of our agenda</u> must be securing Russian cooperation in preventing terrorists from acquiring nukes.
    - Other concerns, such as Russia's backsliding on democracy, must be given lesser priority.
    - A successful working relationship requires that both leaders <u>speak candidly about disagreements</u>—such as plutonium disposal liability—and find solutions.

The Record since 9/11

- In October 2001, Presidents Bush and Putin identified the nexus of terrorists and weapons of mass destruction as the greatest threat to both nations, and pledged "to keep the world's most dangerous technologies out of the hands of the world's most dangerous people."
    - Unfortunately, neither nations' deeds have matched either president's words:
        - In the two years after 9/11, fewer potential nuclear weapons in Russia were secured than in the two years before that attack.
    - Alarming reports of nuclear insecurity in Russia and the former Soviet Union continue to emerge.
        - Nuclear security culture in Russia is weak: reports of guards patrolling without ammunition and doors propped open for convenience.
    - In his February 2005 testimony to Congress, CIA Director Porter Goss gave the intelligence community's best judgment of Russian loose nukes:

- o "There is sufficient material unaccounted for so that it would be possible for those with know-how to construct a nuclear weapon."
- o Senator Rockefeller followed up, asking, "Can you assure the American people that the material missing from Russian nuclear sites has not found its way into terrorist hands?" Goss replied, "No, I can't make that assurance."
- There is also good news:
  - o At Bratislava, Presidents Bush and Putin for the first time accepted personal responsibility for addressing nuclear terrorism and assuring that their governments act urgently.
  - o There is recent evidence of rising Russian consciousness about preventing nuclear terrorism:
    - ■ Russian President Vladimir Putin, "It is important to neutralize the attempts to proliferate weapons of mass destruction," Bratislava Summit, February 24, 2005.
    - ■ Chief of the Russian General Staff Yury Baluyevsky, "Nuclear weapons could soon escape the control of the nuclear powers and become accessible throughout the world, and there is an understanding of this at the political and military level in the United States, Russia, and other members of the nuclear club," *Nezavisimaya Gazeta,* March 2, 2005.
  - o Two years ago, the U.S. pledged $10 billion to the G8 Global Partnership. Unfortunately, actual allocation of these funds is still in its infancy.

What Should be Done Now: An Alternative Strategy
- Move from assistance to partnership.
- Accelerate and strengthen U.S.–Russian cooperation.
  - o Build Russian commitment to sustain high levels of security once international assistance ends.
  - o Agree on what levels of security are needed and what standards should be met.
  - o Decide on specific deadlines for when all loose Russian nuclear weapons and materials will be contained and secured.
  - o Resolve remaining access and liability issues.
  - o Consolidate nuclear stockpiles.
  - o Develop nuclear "security culture."
  - o Exchange "best practices" for securing nukes.
  - o Work together on nuclear security in the rest of the world to ensure that every weapon and every kilogram of material worldwide is secured and accounted for.
- Improve Nunn–Lugar.
  - o Streamline to remove bureaucratic obstacles.
  - o Establish who is in charge.

STRENGTHENING THE NUCLEAR NONPROLIFERATION SYSTEM: MISSING U.S. LEADERSHIP SINCE 9/11

The Growing Danger to America

- In 1962, President John F. Kennedy warned that on the current path there could be 20 nuclear weapons states by the end of the 1970's.
    - Because of initiatives he and successive presidents took to prevent that, <u>today there are only 8 nuclear armed states.</u>
    - The centerpiece of the nonproliferation regime that has constrained the spread of nuclear weapons is the Treaty on the Non-Proliferation of Nuclear Weapons (NPT).
        - In that compact, <u>184 nations have voluntarily rejected nuclear weapons.</u> These include 40 states like Japan, Germany, Sweden, and Singapore that have the technical infrastructure to build nuclear arsenals quickly, if they chose to do so.
        - Associated agreements, including the Nuclear Suppliers Group and the Proliferation Security Initiative, aim to stop the sale of items and technologies that would assist states – or even terrorist groups – in building nuclear weapons.
    - In the aftermath of 9/11, the Security Council passed <u>UNSCR 1540</u>, which <u>forbids states from assisting WMD proliferation by non-state actors</u>, obligates them to enact and enforce laws to prevent such proliferation, and requires countries to establish and enforce controls over sensitive materials and technologies within their borders.
    - Unfortunately, even in this arena, the Bush Administration has demonstrated disdain for international agreements.

The Record since 9/11

- The Bush administration has disparaged the NPT regime, saying it has no value for the "good guys" and is inadequate for the "bad guys" who can either not join or join and quit without penalties.
- But even in its current form the NPT contributes to American security.
    - There are not only "good guys" and "bad guys" but in-betweens, represented in recent history by Ukraine, Kazakstan, Belarus (at the time it signed the NPT), South Africa, Argentina, Brazil, Taiwan, South Korea, and others who turned away from nuclear weapons in part because of the NPT.
    - When the U.S. leads the world against the "bad guys," it can draw upon the support of the NPT signatories.
- Preventing nuclear breakout and terrorism requires a comprehensive U.S. strategy that uses all tools – we cannot afford to write off any of them.
- Yet the current form of the NPT is not adequate and needs U.S.-led revamping.
    - In the view of the majority of 85 nuclear experts surveyed by Senator Lugar, on the current course, 2-5 new nuclear nations will arise in the next decade.
    - The actions of two countries threaten to collapse - or explode - the nonproliferation regime.

- - If Iran goes nuclear under the guise of a civilian program, Egypt might follow, then Saudi Arabia (more likely buying than making) and possibly Syria.
    - If no one stops North Korea from gaining forced entry into the nuclear club, Japan and South Korea might not be far behind. Taiwan will certainly explore its nuclear options.
    - If North Korea and Iran achieve their nuclear ambitions, President Bush will have presided over the collapse of the nonproliferation regime.
  - The opportunity presented at the recent NPT Review Conference to focus international attention on North Korean and Iranian actions that threaten to puncture and even collapse the entire nonproliferation regime was missed by:
    - Walking away from the 13 steps pledge made by the U.S. at the previous NPT Review Conference,
    - Failing to appoint a high-level envoy,
    - Failing to develop an agenda, and
    - Arriving at the meeting in New York without having assembled a coalition of the like-minded.
    - The U.S. found itself as much a target for others' accusations of non-compliance as did Iran.
  - To revitalize the treaty, the U.S. must appreciate that countries can't be bullied into cooperation – they, like we, act in terms of their views of their own self-interest.
  - Countries weighing the utility of having nuclear weapons will stay in the NPT and foreswear nukes for a number of reasons:
    - If the regime is effective in keeping their neighbors from getting the bomb,
    - If the regime provides benefits in access to civilian nuclear technology,
    - If the international nuclear taboo remains strong,
    - If the regime leads to restraint on the part of the nuclear weapon states.
    - If the net balance of other carrots and sticks make such a choice in their interest.
- President Bush gave a speech addressing needed changes to the NPT on February 11, 2004 but – characteristically – there has been little follow-up and no result.

What Should be Done Now: An Alternative Strategy
- The United States should:
  - Adopt four goals as U.S. policy;
  - Develop specific proposals for the U.S. to achieve each goal;
  - Seek international support for each proposal.
- FIRST GOAL: PREVENTING NUCLEAR TERRORISM
  - The NPT was conceived long before 9/11, and even before the Munich Olympics. It deals with possession of nuclear weapons by governments.
  - But the NPT system of the future must also address "proliferation" to terrorists.

- The key to preventing "proliferation" to terrorists is stopping the production of fissile material for weapons and safeguarding all fissile materials everywhere from terrorists.
- This is a new agenda for nonproliferation. Traditional nonproliferation addresses the problem of diversion of fissile material from non-military purposes to military purposes. The new agenda must address diversion from government-sponsored purposes (military or non-military) to non-governments (terrorists).
- India, Pakistan, and Israel are not members of the NPT and cannot be members, but they can be members of a new understanding addressing the new agenda of preventing proliferation to terrorists.
- This new understanding would commit all governments to:
  - Internationally accepted standards of safe custody and control of fissile materials – standards established in the U.S.-Russian Nunn-Lugar program.
  - Joint action to prevent diversion to terrorists (including but not limited to measures being pursued in the G8 initiative, PSI, and UNSCR 1540).
  - Joint planning for humanitarian and strategic response to a nuclear explosion anywhere in the participating states.

- SECOND GOAL: STOPPING THE PROLIFERATION OF URANIUM ENRICHMENT AND PLUTONIUM REPROCESSING CAPABILITY
  - Traditionally the NPT has permitted and even encouraged the "peaceful atom," meaning in particular that parties may enrich uranium and reprocess plutonium. Every aspect of international policy calls for departure from this traditional understanding of the NPT.
    - Nonproliferation. Enrichment and reprocessing allow nations to obtain the critical ingredients of a nuclear weapons capability – fissile material – within the treaty and then "break out" of the treaty to full weapons capability.
    - Counterterrorism. After 9/11, U.S. policy must reflect the fact that every kilogram of uranium or plutonium made anywhere poses a potential danger of nuclear terrorism through theft, sale, or diversion.
    - Energy economics. There is no economic reason for reprocessing or for proliferating uranium enrichment capability today or for decades to come – a fact that was not clear when the NPT was first signed.
    - Energy security. The world will need more nuclear power to fuel a growing demand for electricity without increasing dependence on fossil fuel. The explosion of a nuclear bomb anywhere in the world will cause populations to demand a halt to this needed expansion of nuclear power.
    - Global warming. Nuclear power is a key part of any strategy to contain carbon dioxide from burning fossil fuels. Once again, a single nuclear explosion will halt the expansion of peaceful nuclear power.
  - The United States should oppose the proliferation of enrichment and reprocessing capabilities. In return for foregoing such facilities, countries would be assured access to fuel services by existing providers of such services.

- President Bush's proposal stops short of opposing all such proliferation of enrichment and reprocessing, and he has failed to obtain international agreement even to his limited proposal.
- THIRD GOAL: STRENGTHENING VERIFICATION AND COMPLIANCE OF THE NPT
  - The NPT system needs better means to detect and punish cheating.
  - To detect cheating:
    - The U.S. should provide further financial and technical aid to the IAEA, and to share intelligence with the IAEA wherever possible;
    - The IAEA's inspection rights, obligations, and procedures should be extended from fissile material-producing capabilities to all nuclear weapons-related activities;
    - The U.S. should more actively promote the universal adoption of the Agreed Protocol.
  - To ensure prompt resolution of suspected cheating, states under suspicion should:
    - Have their membership on the IAEA Board of Governors suspended;
    - Have their rights to peaceful nuclear cooperation suspended;
    - Be subject to inspections that go beyond even the Agreed Protocol.
  - To deter and punish cheating, violators who wish to remain members of the NPT automatically:
    - Lose the right to peaceful nuclear cooperation for a period of time;
    - Become subject to extra IAEA inspections in perpetuity.
  - Uncorrected cheating invites the cheater's facilities to physical attack.
- FOURTH GOAL: PREVENTING "BREAKOUT" OF THE NPT
  - NPT members should not be permitted to take their nuclear programs right up to the line of compliance and then withdraw from the Treaty and "break out" to a nuclear weapons capability.
  - The fuel cycle provisions of the SECOND GOAL go a long way in this direction.
  - But additional measures can be taken. Withdrawal should automatically trigger the following:
    - The UNSC takes the matter of withdrawal up under Chapter VII of the UN Charter;
    - Withdrawing states forfeit any technology they obtained for "peaceful purposes" during their period of membership;
    - During the 90-day period between the announcement of withdrawal and the effective withdrawal date (this period is clearly stated in the Treaty), withdrawing states would be subject to more intrusive inspections than those provided by the Agreed Protocol (to permit the UNSC to make an assessment of their intentions). If it is found during this period of intensive inspection that the state violated its obligations during the time of its membership, it shall, despite its intention to withdraw, nevertheless be treated as though it violated the NPT.

Real Security:
Protecting America and Restoring Our Leadership in the World

War on Terror: Additional Resources

Terrorism

2006 National Security Briefing Book, **Foreign Policy Leadership Council, February 2006. Chapter 3: Terrorism.** This briefing book outlines key issues and talking points regarding weapons of mass destruction, including the Bush Administration's record on addressing the threats of nuclear terrorism, Iran, North Korea, biological and chemical weapons and nonproliferation initiatives. It also provides recommendations for addressing these challenges.

Combating Al Qaeda and the Militant Islamic Threat, **Bruce Hoffman, Testimony presented to the House Armed Services Committee, Subcommittee on Terrorism, Unconventional Threats and Capabilities on February 16, 2006.** Mr. Hoffman's testimony outlines U.S. progress in the war on terrorism, examines evolving threat of al Qaeda and its affiliated networks and provides recommendations for more effectively addressing its challenge to U.S. national security and global stability. [Available at: http://www.rand.org/pubs/testimonies/2006/RAND_CT255.pdf]

"Blowback Revisited." Peter Bergen, *Foreign Affairs,* **November 1, 2005.** This article examines the likely consequences of the war in Iraq on the war on terrorism, warning that "today's insurgents in Iraq are tomorrow's terrorists." [Available at: http://www.newamerica.net/index.cfm?pg=article&DocID=2648]

Weapons of Mass Destruction

The Race to Secure Russia's Loose Nukes: Progress Since 9/11, **Brian Finlay and Andrew Grotto, Henry L. Stimson Center and the Center for American Progress.** This report analyzes U.S. progress in implementing the 2001 Cutler-Baker bipartisan Task Force recommendations for dealing with Russia's so-called "loose nukes" challenge. It provides recommendations for dealing with shortcomings in implementation. [Available at: http://www.stimson.org/ctr/pdf/LooseNukes.pdf]

Securing the Bomb 2005, **Matthew Bunn and Anthony Wier, The Nuclear Threat Initiative, May 2005.** Building on three previous annual reports, this new Nuclear Threat Initiative (NTO)-commissioned report evaluates current efforts and recommends new actions to more effectively prevent nuclear terrorism. It finds that while the United States and other countries laid important foundations for an accelerated effort to prevent nuclear terrorism in the last year, sustained presidential leadership will be needed to win the race to lock down the world's nuclear stockpiles before terrorists and thieves can get

to them. [Executive summary and full report available at:
http://www.nti.org/e_research/cnwm/overview/cnwm_home.asp]

Iran

**"Iran: Is There a Way Out of the Nuclear Impasse?" International Crisis Group. 23
February 2006.** This report provides a background and examines the current Iranian
nuclear dilemma, from the perspective of Teheran, the U.S., Europe, Moscow, Beijing
and the IAEA. It explores current EU-led diplomatic initiatives, outlines alternate
scenarios for a negotiated compromise, and offers specific policy recommendations.
[Available at:
http://www.crisisgroup.org/library/documents/middle_east___north_africa/iraq_iran_gulf
/51_iran_is_there_a_way_out_of_the_nuclear_impasse.pdf]

A Nuclear Iran: Challenges and Responses, **Ray Takeyh, The Council on Foreign
Relations, March 2, 2006.** Takeyh examines the challenge of Iran's nuclear ambitions
and potential U.S. and international responses. He argues that it "is neither inevitable nor
absolute that Iran will become the next member of the nuclear club, as its internal debates
are real and its course of actions is still unsettled. The international community and the
United States will have an immeasurable impact on Iran's nuclear future. A more
imaginative U.S. diplomacy can still prevent Iran from crossing the nuclear threshold and
assembling a bomb." [Available at: http://www.cfr.org/publication/10008/]

"Taking on Teheran" by Kenneth Pollack and Ray Takeyh, *Foreign Affairs*,
March/April 2005. "If Washington wants to derail Iran's nuclear program, it must take
advantage of a split in Tehran between hard-liners, who care mostly about security, and
pragmatists, who want to fix Iran's ailing economy. By promising strong rewards for
compliance and severe penalties for defiance, Washington can strengthen the pragmatists'
case that Tehran should choose butter over bombs." [Available at:
http://www.foreignaffairs.org/20050301faessay84204/kenneth-pollack-ray-takeyh/taking-
on-tehran.html]

Iran: U.S. Concerns and Policy Responses, **Kenneth Katzman, Congressional
Research Service, March 20, 2006.** This report provides a comprehensive overview of
Iran's WMD programs, the country's political landscape and U.S. policy options for
addressing its nuclear activities. [Available at:
http://www.congress.gov/erp/rl/pdf/RL32048.pdf]

Iran's Nuclear Program: Recent Developments. **Congressional Research Service,
February 28, 2006.** This report provides a background Iran's nuclear program and
outlines IAEA and UN Security Council reactions to its nuclear activities. [Available at:
http://www.congress.gov/erp/rs/pdf/RS21592.pdf]

North Korea

"Six Party Talks: False Start or a Case for Optimism", Charles L. Pritchard, The Brookings Institution, December 1, 2005. This paper provides a background of the Six Party Talks with North Korea and an updated analysis of the fourth round of negotiations, held in November, 2005. It offers insight into the diplomatic challenges the U.S. faces in dealing with North Korea's nuclear program. [Available at: http://www.brookings.edu/fp/cnaps/events/20051201presentation.pdf]

"No Good Choices--The Implications of a Nuclear North Korea," Testimony by Carnegie Deputy Director for Nonproliferation Jon Wolfsthal to the U.S. House of Representatives International Relations Committee Joint Hearing of the Subcommittees on Asia and the Pacific and on International Terrorism and Nonproliferation, 17 February 2005. This testimony looks at: 1.) what we know and do not know about North Korea's nuclear capabilities and 2.) the larger role of the US in East Asia. "Current US policy toward the North is based on a set of assumptions about how our partners in the region see us and our objectives, and where their key interests lie. On almost all counts, the assumptions of the current administration in the region appear questionable and put American interests in long-term jeopardy." [Available at: http://wwwc.house.gov/international_relations/109/wol021705.htm]

North Korea's Nuclear Weapons Program, Larry A. Niksch, Congressional Research Service, February 21, 2006. This report outlines the most recent developments in North Korea's nuclear program and provides a background and analysis of relevant issues: the Bush Administration's policy toward North Korea, including the Six Party Talks, North Korea's policy and diplomatic strategy, and the state of North Korea's nuclear weapons program. It also documents previous administration policy and diplomatic agreements with North Korea, including the Agreed Framework and amending agreements. [Available at: http://www.congress.gov/erp/ib/pdf/IB91141.pdf]

India

U.S. Nuclear Cooperation with India: Issues for Congress. Sharon Squassoni, Congressional Research Service, March 3, 2006. This report provides a background on U.S.-India nuclear cooperation and examines the potential impact of the March 2, 2006 agreement negotiated between the U.S. and Indian government. It examines the potential impact of this deal on U.S. nonproliferation efforts and the international nonproliferation regime. The report also outlines the next steps in the process and the key considerations for Congress in addressing this issue. [Available at: http://www.congress.gov/erp/rl/pdf/RL33016.pdf]

"U.S.-India nuclear deal falls short," Robert J. Einhorn, *San Francisco Chronicle*, March 17, 2006. Robert Einhorn, former Assistant Secretary of State for Nonproliferation and current CSIS expert, argues that the U.S.-India nuclear deal, as brokered on March 2, 2006, falls short of U.S. nonproliferation objectives and would weaken the international nonproliferation regime. He calls on Congress to push for an agreement that would strengthen nonproliferation efforts. [Available at: http://www.sfgate.com/cgi-bin/article.cgi?file=/chronicle/archive/2006/03/17/EDGU9GJFJ11.DTL]

***Clarifying the Record on the July 18 Proposal for Nuclear Cooperation with India Joint Letter from Arms Control and Nonproliferation Experts to Members of Congress,* February 14, 2006.** This memo outlines the potential international security and nonproliferation implications of U.S.-India nuclear cooperation. It lists key issues for Congressional consideration to ensure that a U.S.-India deal strengthens the international nonproliferation regime.
http://www.armscontrol.org/pdf/20060214_India_Clarifying_Responses.pdf

"India's Gas Centrifuge Program: Stopping Illicit Procurement and the Leakage of Technical Centrifuge Know-How," David Albright and Susan Basu, Institute for Science and International Security (ISIS), March 10, 2006. This ISIS report challenges Indian nuclear and government officials' claims that the country has an "impeccable" nonproliferation record. It details an active, covert Indian program for uranium enrichment and documents leaks of sensitive nuclear technology. In light of these findings, it calls on the U.S. to take the steps necessary to ensure that the Indian government stops these illicit activities before finalizing a deal for nuclear cooperation. [Available at: http://www.isis-online.org/publications/southasia/indianprocurement.pdf]

Real Security:
Protecting America and Restoring Our Leadership in the World

HOMELAND SECURITY

After September 11, Americans trusted President Bush to take the steps necessary to keep our country safe. Since then, inadequate planning and incompetent policies have failed to make Americans as safe as we should be.

In July 2004, the independent, bipartisan 9/11 Commission submitted to Congress and the nation a report containing 41 recommendations on how to improve intelligence operations and homeland security. In December 2004, Congress enacted the Intelligence Reform Act (or "the 9/11 Act") authorizing several of these recommendations. However, the Bush Administration and the Republican-led Congress have failed to live up to the commitments made in the 9/11 Act. Almost every single one of the commitments made in the 9/11 Act on homeland security have been significantly underfunded. In addition, there has been a severe lack of leadership and competency at the Department of Homeland Security – culminating in the failed response to Hurricane Katrina.

On December 5, 2005, when the 9/11 Commission issued its final report card, it gave the Bush Administration and the Republican-led Congress a series of C's, D's, and F's on many areas in homeland security. These areas include port security, border security, aviation security, chemical plant security, and first responders.

Democrats believe that the government's most important responsibility is to "provide for the common defense" and have an aggressive, robust plan to secure our homeland.

To Protect America from Terrorism and Natural Disasters, Democrats will:

- Immediately implement the recommendations of the independent, bipartisan 9/11 Commission including securing national borders, ports, airports and mass transit systems.

- Screen 100% of containers and cargo bound for the U.S. in ships or airplanes at the point of origin and safeguard America's nuclear and chemical plants, and food and water supplies.

- Prevent outsourcing of critical components of our national security infrastructure -- such as ports, airports and mass transit -- to foreign interests that put America at risk.

- Provide firefighters, emergency medical workers, police officers, and other workers on the front lines with the training, staffing, equipment and cutting-edge technology they need.

- Protect America from biological terrorism and pandemics, including the Avian flu, by investing in the public health infrastructure and training public health workers.

Bush/Republican Record on Homeland Security

"We are not as safe as we need to be… There are far too many C's, D's, and F's in the report card we will issue today. Many obvious steps that the American people assume have been completed, have not been. … Some of these failures are shocking. … We are frustrated by the lack of urgency about fixing these problems."
- 9/11 Commission Chair Thomas Kean and Vice-Chair Lee Hamilton, 12/5/05

Port Security

9/11 commission gives Washington Republicans a "D" on screening cargo, including at ports. The 9/11 Commission report concluded that terrorists have "the opportunity to do harm as great or greater in maritime and surface transportation" than the 9/11 terrorist attacks. And yet the Bush Administration and the Republican-led Congress have done little on port security. As a result, in the report card it issued in December 2005, the 9/11 Commission gave Washington Republicans a "D" on screening cargo, including at ports.

Four and a half years after 9/11, <u>only 6 percent</u> of containers entering U.S. ports are screened. A weapon of mass destruction detonated in a container at a seaport could cause tremendous numbers of casualties, and an estimated economic loss ranging from $58 billion to $1 trillion. And yet, due to the neglect of Washington Republicans on port security, only 6 percent of containers entering U.S. seaports are currently being screened.

Four and a half years after 9/11, <u>fewer than half</u> of the ports of entry have radiation portal monitors. The 9/11 Commission report concluded that terrorists have the "opportunity to do harm as great or greater in maritime and surface transportation" than the 9/11 attacks. And yet Washington Republicans have been slow to deploy radiation portal monitors – at both sea and land ports of entry. Under the Administration's policy, all ports of entry wouldn't have radiation portal monitors until 2011.

Washington Republicans have been grossly underfunding port security. Over the last five years, the Republican-controlled Congress has only appropriated about $800 million for port security grants – whereas the Coast Guard has stated that $5.4 billion is needed for enhancing port security over 10 years. Furthermore, in his FY 2007 budget, President Bush proposes <u>eliminating</u> the $173 million Port Security Grant program by rolling these grants into a larger grant program – thereby forcing port officials to compete for funding against other critical infrastructure.

First Responders

9/11 commission gives Washington Republicans an "F" on improving communications for first responders. In the 9/11 Commission's December 2005 report card, Washington Republicans got an "F" on communications for first responders. Indeed, Hurricane Katrina exposed that, four years after 9/11, little progress has been made in creating a system where police, fire and emergency medical service departments can communicate with each other.

President Bush is proposing <u>eliminating</u> the COPS Interoperable Communications Grant program. Despite the fact that first responders still can't communicate with each other, the President's FY 2007 budget proposes eliminating the very popular and successful COPS Interoperable Communications Grant program which is charged with awarding technology grants to law enforcement agencies for enhancing interoperability.

Four and a half years after 9/11, first responders still don't have the training and equipment they need. Washington Republicans have let down our first responders. Over the last four years, Republicans have slashed First Responder Grants in the Homeland Security Department by 59 percent – from $2.3 billion in FY 2003 to $941 million in FY 2006. They have also slashed the COPS program in the Justice Department, which also provides equipment and training for police officers. They have slashed COPS funding by 51 percent – from $978 million in FY 2002 to $478 million in FY 2006. Now, the President's budget for FY 2007 sets the COPS program on the path for elimination – proposing an additional cut of 79 percent.

Border Security

9/11 Commission gives Washington Republicans a "D" on international collaboration on border security. In the 9/11 Commission's December 2005 report card, Washington Republicans got a "D" on international collaboration on border security. The commission points out that there has been no systematic diplomatic effort to work with other countries on shared terrorist watchlists – to ensure terrorists can't get across our borders.

There are 1,000 fewer additional Border Patrol Agents than were promised in the 9/11 Act. The Republican Congress has broken the promises it made on funding additional Border Patrol Agents, immigration enforcement agents and detention beds. Specifically, in 2004, Congress enacted the Intelligence Reforms Act (or the "9/11 Act"; PL 108-458), which mandated an additional 2,000 Border Patrol agents being hired over each of the next five years. And yet, for FY 2006, the Republican-led Congress funded only 1,000 additional agents. The 9/11 Act also mandated an additional 800 immigration enforcement agents over each of the next five years. And yet, for FY 2006, the Congress funded only 350 additional agents. The Act also mandated an additional 8,000 detention beds. Yet, for FY 2006, the Congress funded only 1,800 additional detention beds.

Aviation Security

9/11 commission gives Washington Republicans an "F" on airline passenger pre-screening. In the 9/11 Commission's December 2005 report card, Washington Republicans got an "F" on airline passenger pre-screening. Four and a half years after 9/11, there is still not a unified terrorist watch list for screening airline passengers.

Four and a half years after 9/11, most air cargo is still not screened. Washington Republicans have still not made the investments necessary to ensure that air cargo carried on passenger aircraft is screened for explosives. In addition, the Republican-led Congress continues to severely underfund the installation of in-line explosive detection systems at airports across the country and needed R&D for improved explosive detection systems.

Rail and Transit Security

Since 9/11, little has been done to enhance security for our rail and transit systems. Coordinated and timed bombings in London and Madrid are the latest example of the fact that from 1998 to 2003, there were 181 terrorist attacks on rail targets worldwide. And yet Republicans have provided only $600 million of the estimated $6 billion needed to improve transit security since 9/11. And they have provided only $145 million for rail security since 9/11. Now, in his FY 2007 budget, President Bush proposes eliminating the $150 million Rail and Transit Security Grant program by rolling these grants into a larger grant program.

Chemical Plant Security

9/11 commission gives Washington Republicans a "D" for security for critical infrastructure, including chemical plants. In the 9/11 Commission's December 2005 report card, Washington Republicans got a "D" on chemical plant security. Four and a half years after 9/11, the Administration has still <u>failed</u> to issue any security standards for chemical plants. Belatedly, on March 21, Secretary Chertoff announced that the time has come for the Federal Government to have a role in chemical plant security – but continues to insist on only voluntary compliance. There are over 3,000 chemical facilities where a toxic release could threaten over 10,000 people.

Bioterrorism/Avian Flu

Since 9/11, Republicans have done too little on combating bioterrorism and investing in our public health infrastructure. Since 9/11, Republicans have failed to make key investments to better prepare for bioterrorism and to make our public health infrastructure stronger. Indeed, for FY 2006, Republicans cut funding for grants to local health departments for preparedness against bioterrorism by $96 million or 11 percent. Last year, the GOP Congress also only provided $3.8 billion of the $7.1 billion that the President had requested for avian flu.

Democratic Record on Homeland Security

Since 9/11, Democrats have been fighting to improve the nation's efforts on homeland security – attempting to get the Republican-led Congress and the Bush Administration to address the numerous gaps in the nation's security. In almost every case, Democratic efforts to close gaps in our security here at home have been rebuffed by the Republicans; as a result the GOP has received failing grades on homeland security from the 9/11 Commission.

Overall Homeland Security

Senate Democrats have fought to make homeland security a top priority. Since 9/11, Senate Democrats have repeatedly tried to make homeland security a top budget priority. For example, Sen. Joe Lieberman (D-CT) offered an amendment to the FY 2006 Budget Resolution to provide an additional $8 billion for homeland security, including $1.6 billion for first responders, $1 billion for transit and rail security, $1 billion for enhanced bioterrorism preparedness, $400 million for Port Security Grants, and $150 million for chemical security. Republicans defeated the amendment by a vote of 43 to 53. (*Senate Vote #59*, 3/16/06)

House Democrats have also fought to make homeland security a top priority. House Democrats have also repeatedly fought for homeland security as a top priority. For example, Rep. Bennie Thompson (D-MS) offered a Democratic substitute to the FY 2006 Homeland Security Authorization. The substitute included an additional $6.9 billion for homeland security, including meeting the commitments of the 9/11 Act, such as $380 million to ensure 2,000 additional Border Patrol agents; $160 million for securing air cargo; and $92 million for radiation portal monitors. Republicans defeated the substitute by a vote of 196 to 230. (*2005 House Vote #187*, 5/18/05)

Port Security

House Democrats have fought for port security. Since 9/11, House Democrats have repeatedly tried to increase investments in port security. For example, Rep. Martin Sabo (D-MN) offered an amendment to the FY 2006 Supplemental Appropriations bill to increase port security funding by $825 million. The amendment includes $400 million to place radiation portal monitors at all U.S. ports of entry. Republicans defeated the Sabo amendment by a vote of 208 to 210. (*2006 House Vote #56*, 3/16/06)

Senate Democrats have also fought for port security. Senate Democrats have also repeatedly fought to increase port security investments. For example, Sen. Patty Murray (D-WA) offered an amendment to the FY 2005 Homeland Security Appropriations bill to increase funding for Port Security Grants by $300 million. Republicans blocked the amendment, by a vote of 45 to 49. (*2004 Senate Vote #171*, 9/9/04)

First Responders

Senate Democrats have fought for first responders. Since 9/11, Senate Democrats have repeatedly tried to increase investments in first responders. For example, Sen. Debbie Stabenow (D-MI) offered an amendment to the FY 2006 Budget Resolution to invest $5 billion to provide interoperable communications equipment for first responders. Republicans rejected the amendment by a vote of 43 to 55. (*2006 Senate Vote #45*, 3/15/06)

House Democrats have also fought for first responders. House Democrats have also repeatedly fought to increase first responder investments. For example, Rep. David Obey (D-WI) offered a motion to recommit the FY 2003 Continuing Appropriations bill, to add provisions ensuring $3.5 billion in new money for the nation's first responders. The President had requested only $1 billion in new money for first responders in his FY 2003 budget. Republicans defeated the motion to recommit by a vote of 201 to 222. (*2003 House Vote #16*, 1/28/03)

Border Security

House Democrats have fought for border security. Since 9/11, House Democrats have repeatedly tried to increase investments in border security. For example, Rep. David Obey (D-WI) offered a motion to recommit the conference report on FY 2005 Supplemental Appropriations bill with instructions to add $284 million to fund an additional 550 Border Patrol agents, an additional 200 immigration agents, and unmanned border aerial vehicles. Republicans defeated the motion to recommit by a vote of 201 to 225. (*2005 House Vote #160*, 5/5/05)

Senate Democrats have also fought for border security. Senate Democrats have also repeatedly fought to increase border security investments. For example, Sen. Robert Byrd (D-WV) offered an amendment to the FY 2005 Supplemental Appropriations bill to increase funding for border security by $390 million, providing for the hiring of additional Border Patrol agents and the operation of unmanned aerial vehicles. With support from 21 Republicans, Democrats succeeded in adopting the Byrd amendment – by a vote of 65 to 34. (2005 Senate Vote #105, 4/20/05) However, most of this additional border security funding was removed by the GOP in conference.

Aviation Security

Senate Democrats have fought for aviation security. Since 9/11, Senate Democrats have repeatedly tried to increase investments in aviation security. For example, Sen. Chuck Schumer (D-NY) offered an amendment to the FY 2006 Homeland Security Appropriations bill to provide $302 million for improved screening of cargo carried on commercial airliners. Republicans blocked the amendment by a vote of 45 to 53. (*2005 Senate Vote #180*, 7/14/05)

House Democrats have also fought for aviation security. House Democrats have also repeatedly fought to increase aviation security investments. For example, Rep. Bennie Thompson (D-MS) offered a motion to recommit the FY 2006 Homeland Security Authorization with instructions to authorize $400 million more in FY 2006 for in-line checked baggage screening system installations as well as to require that all air cargo on passenger planes be screened within three years. Republicans rejected the motion to recommit by a vote of 199 to 228. (*2005 House Vote #188*, 5/18/05)

Rail and Transit Security

Senate Democrats have fought for rail and transit security. Since 9/11, Senate Democrats have repeatedly tried to increase investments in rail and transit security. For example, Sen. Robert Byrd (D-WV) offered an amendment to the FY 2006 Homeland Security Appropriations bill to provide $1.2 billion for transit security grants and $265 million for intercity rail transportation. Republicans blocked the amendment by a vote of 43 to 55. (*2005 Senate Vote #184*, 7/14/05)

House Democrats have also fought for rail and transit security. House Democrats have also repeatedly fought to increase rail and transit security investments. For example, Rep. Bennie

Thompson (D-MS) offered a Democratic substitute to the FY 2006 Homeland Security Authorization bill. This substitute included key provisions to bolster rail and transit security – including a three-year $2.8 billion grant program to improve transit security and a three-year $1 billion program to improve rail security. Republicans defeated the substitute by a vote of 196 to 230. (*2005 House Vote #187*, 5/18/05)

Rhetoric vs. Reality on Homeland Security

Rhetoric: **"We've done a lot of work at our seaports. … We've made dramatic advancements in port security since September 11th."** [President Bush, 7/20/05]

Reality: The Bush Administration has seriously neglected port security:
- Four and a half years after 9/11, <u>only 6 percent</u> of cargo containers entering U.S. seaports are being screened.
- Four and a half years after 9/11, <u>fewer than half</u> of the U.S. ports of entry have radiation portal monitors – to detect nuclear materials.
- Four and a half years after 9/11, U.S. personnel are only screening containers at <u>43 of the 140 overseas ports</u> shipping directly to the U.S.
- President Bush is proposing <u>eliminating</u> Port Security Grants in his FY 2007 budget – rolling them into a larger grant program.

Rhetoric: **"The Department of Homeland Security has improved airline security."** [President Bush, 1/11/05]

Reality: The Bush Administration has failed to take critically important steps on airline security:
- Four and a half years after 9/11, most air cargo carried on passenger aircraft is still not screened for explosives.
- The Bush Administration has failed to implement the 9/11 Commission's recommendation to quickly complete the installation of in-line explosive detection systems at airports across the country.
- The Bush Administration has failed to implement the 9/11 Commission's recommendation to increase R& D on improved explosive detection systems.

Rhetoric: **"We're protecting our nation's … transportation systems."** [President Bush, 7/11/05]

Reality: The Bush Administration has seriously neglected transit and rail security:
- Under the Bush Administration, since 9/11, for every seven dollars we spend on security for an airline passenger, we spend just a penny for a mass transit passenger.
- Since 9/11, under the Bush Administration, only $600 million of the estimated $6 billion needed has been provided for transit security.
- Since 9/11, under the Bush Administration, only $145 million has been provided for rail security.
- President Bush is proposing <u>eliminating</u> Rail and Transit Security Grants in his FY 2007 budget – rolling them into a larger grant program.

Rhetoric: **"The Department of Homeland Security has taken action to strengthen the hand of our partners in state and local law enforcement. … We're giving them the tools and information they need to do their jobs."** [President Bush, 3/3/05]

Reality: The Bush Administration has been slashing funding for first responders.
- Under the Bush Administration, funding for First Responder Grants in the Department of Homeland Security has been slashed by 59 percent – from $2.3 billion in FY 2003 to $941 million in FY 2006.

- Under the Bush Administration, funding for the COPS program in the Department of Justice has been slashed by 51 percent – from $978 million in FY 2002 to $478 million in FY 2006.
- In his FY 2007 budget, President Bush proposes setting the COPS program on the path for elimination – proposing an additional cut of 79 percent.

Critics of the Bush/Republican Record
On Homeland Security

9/11 Commission Chairman Thomas Kean and Vice-Chair Lee Hamilton: "We are not as safe as we need to be… There are far too many C's, D's and F's in the report card [on homeland security] we will issue today. Many obvious steps that the American people assume have been completed, have not been. … Some of these failures are shocking. Four years after 9/11: It is scandalous that police and firefighters in large cities still cannot communicate reliably in a major crisis. And it is scandalous that airline passengers are still not screened against all names on the terrorist watchlist." [Statement of Thomas Kean and Lee Hamilton on releasing 9/11 Commission's report card, 12/5/05]

Stephen Flynn, a Council on Foreign Relations fellow and retired Coast Guard commander, on homeland security overall: "How far have we come since 9/11? The answer is not very far at all." [Council on Foreign Relations interview with Stephen Flynn, 12/21/05]

Stephen Flynn, on port security: "Port security today is a house of cards. For each of the [port security] programs, the bar is not very high and there is very little in the way of verification. The result is it is not much of an effective deterrent." [*New York Times*, 2/26/06]

John Lehman, a 9/11 Commissioner and a Secretary of the Navy under President Reagan: "The [Bush] Administration just does not seem to get it. It appears to have a childlike belief that creating a new bureaucracy is the solution to every problem. Creation of the Department of Homeland Security [DHS] has not improved our homeland intelligence. The bureaucratic method was amply demonstrated when DHS held 150 firefighters for three days in Atlanta while people died in New Orleans, so that the firefighters could be given the requisite instruction in avoiding sexual harassment. That's all about process, not results." [Lehman op-ed, "Getting Spy Reform Wrong," *Washington Post*, 11/16/05]

James Thompson, a 9/11 Commissioner and a former Republican governor of Illinois: "In July 2004, the Sept. 11 commission made 41 urgent recommendations to prevent and prepare for terrorist attacks. These recommendations flowed directly from our investigation of Sept. 11, 2001, and the failures that allowed the terrorists' plot to succeed. Earlier this month, the 10 former commissioners came together for the last time, to issue a 'report card' grading action on those reforms. The results were dismal: five F's, 12 D's, nine C's and only one A (an A-minus). Progress in many important areas has been slow or non-existent. While the terrorists are learning and adapting, we have been moving at a bureaucratic crawl." [Thompson op-ed, "Terrorists Will Strike Again," *Chicago Tribune*, 12/16/05]

Fred Fielding, a 9/11 Commissioner and a White House Counsel under President Nixon: "Overall progress to date has been disappointing. … For us to win this race, we must quicken the pace." [*San Francisco Chronicle*, 12/6/05]

Real Security:
Protecting America and Restoring Our Leadership in the World

Homeland Security: Additional Resources

The following web sites offer valuable resources on Homeland Security issues:

Center for Strategic and International Studies (www.csis.org) In particular:
  - ➤ *The Challenge of Biological Terrorism* **by Anthony Cordesman, 12/05.** This report provides an assessment of biological terrorism--balancing threats, probabilities, costs, and priorities. [Available at: http://www.csis.org/component/option,com_csis_pubs/task,view/id,2650/]

The Center for American Progress (www.americanprogress.org) In particular:
  - ➤ *Integrated Power*, **6/05.** Includes a section on securing the homeland. [Available at: http://www.americanprogress.org/site/apps/nl/content3.asp?c=biJRJ8OVF&b=681085&ct=936891]

Homeland Security Affairs: **The Journal of the Center for Homeland Defense and Security** (http://www.hsaj.org/hsa/)

A Failure of Initiative: The Final Report of the Select Bipartisan Committee to Investigate the Preparation for and Response to Hurricane Katrina, **Select Bipartisan Committee to Investigate the Preparation for and Response to Hurricane Katrina.** [Available at: http://katrina.house.gov/]

Hurricane Katrina: Recommendations for Reform, Hearing of the Senate Governmental Affairs Committee, 3/8/06. This hearing focuses on reforming FEMA and emergency response. [Available at: http://hsgac.senate.gov/index.cfm?Fuseaction=Hearings.Detail&HearingID=330]

"Port Security is Still a House of Cards" by Stephen E. Flynn, *Far Eastern Economic Review.* A review of the problems surrounding port security. [Available at: http://www.feer.com/articles1/2006/0601/free/p005.html]

"The Next Pandemic," by Laurie Garrett, *Foreign Affairs*, **July/August 2005.** A look at what might happen if the Avian Influenza virus becomes capable of human-to-human transmission and retains its extraordinary potency. [Available at: http://www.foreignaffairs.org/20050701faessay84401/laurie-garrett/the-next-pandemic.html]

STATE IMPACT OF BUSH 2007 BUDGET CUTS:
ELIMINATING LAW ENFORCEMENT TERRORISM PREVENTION GRANTS

STATE	FUNDING CUT
Alabama	$6,432,290
Alaska	$3,406,760
Arizona	$7,280,630
Arkansas	$5,038,073
California	$30,768,660
Colorado	$6,471,512
Connecticut	$5,633,181
Delaware	$3,539,246
DC	$3,339,656
Florida	$16,264,891
Georgia	$9,718,613
Hawaii	$3,884,939
Idaho	$3,970,337
Illinois	$12,835,959
Indiana	$7,763,554
Iowa	$5,209,576
Kansas	$5,036,340
Kentucky	$6,131,518
Louisiana	$6,428,819
Maine	$3,922,735
Maryland	$7,224,154
Massachusetts	$7,950,319
Michigan	$10,814,538
Minnesota	$6,871,064
Mississippi	$5,160,264
Missouri	$7,377,769
Montana	$3,617,894
Nebraska	$4,263,280
Nevada	$4,657,472
New Hampshire	$3,908,565
New Jersey	$9,682,232
New Mexico	$4,369,571
New York	$17,970,155
North Carolina	$9,500,675
North Dakota	$3,394,993
Ohio	$11,879,471
Oklahoma	$5,655,300
Oregon	$5,693,052
Pennsylvania	$12,609,677
Rhode Island	$3,742,422
South Carolina	$6,154,552
South Dakota	$3,497,474
Tennessee	$7,485,584
Texas	$20,270,283
Utah	$4,744,118
Vermont	$3,383,424
Virginia	$8,698,787
Washington	$7,713,129
West Virginia	$4,319,097
Wisconsin	$7,195,398
Wyoming	$3,290,846

SOURCE: Department of Homeland Security

Real Security:
Protecting America and Restoring Our Leadership in the World

IRAQ

In March 2003, President Bush rushed to war in Iraq based on manipulated intelligence and rosy assessments of a quick victory. As we start the fourth year of this war, the American people now know that the Administration misstated the threat posed by Saddam Hussein, did not listen to military leaders about what it would take to win, did not have a clear plan to win the peace, and still has no strategy to stabilize Iraq and begin the responsible redeployment of our troops there.

The Bush Administration's incompetence in Iraq has inflicted a heavy toll on our troops and taxpayers: more than 2,300 U.S. troops have been killed; over 17,000 have been wounded in Iraq; the direct cost of the Iraq war on U.S. taxpayers will reach at least $320 billion this year and estimates indicate ongoing operations are costing roughly $2 billion per week. Our troops and their families deserve better.

To Honor the Sacrifice of Our Troops, Democrats will:

- Ensure 2006 is a year of significant transition to full Iraqi sovereignty, with the Iraqis assuming primary responsibility for securing and governing their country and with the responsible redeployment of U.S. forces.

- Insist that Iraqis make the political compromises necessary to unite their country and defeat the insurgency; promote regional diplomacy; and strongly encourage our allies and other nations to play a constructive role.

- Hold the Bush Administration accountable for its manipulated pre-war intelligence, poor planning and contracting abuses that have placed our troops at greater risk and wasted billions of taxpayer dollars.

Bush/Republican Record on Iraq

Security:

Problems Persist with Iraqi Security Forces:

- Despite the fact that we have just entered the fourth year of the war and billions have been spent to train Iraqi forces, there are no Iraqi Security Force (ISF) battalions capable of operating without U.S. assistance. [Department of Defense's (DoD) "Measuring Stability and Security in Iraq" Report, 2/06, 10/05; Testimony of General John Abizaid to the Senate Armed Services Committee, 9/29/05]

- U.S. troops are still on the front lines in the most dangerous places: about 60% of all U.S. military deaths have occurred in 2 of the most dangerous provinces: Al Anbar and Baghdad. [Anthony Cordesman, "Iraq's Evolving Insurgency," 2/2/06]

- Iraqi troops have primary responsibility for less than 20 percent of the country overall. [Department of Defense's (DoD) "Measuring Stability and Security in Iraq" Report, 2/06]

- The reliability of Iraqi security forces remains questionable. Militia members are included within the Iraqi security forces, and they remain unchecked, which remains a major obstacle to maintaining law and order in Iraq. [*Reuters*, 3/10/06; *Washington Post*, 2/28/06]

- The U.S. has been holding back the best weapons from Iraqi forces mainly because "Iraqi troops have a reputation for revolving-door enlistments, failure to report for duty and—at times—horrific incompetence." [*Newsweek*, 2/20/06]

Strength of the Iraqi Insurgency Increases:

- Since November 2003, the insurgency has grown from 5,000 fighters to 15,000-20,000 fighters. [Brookings Iraq Index, 3/20/06]

- Insurgent attacks number 75 daily. [Brookings Iraq Index, 3/20/06]

- According to Iraqi officials, insurgent attacks have cost Iraq at least $11 billion. [Anthony Cordesman, "Iraq's Evolving Insurgency," 2/2/06]

Heightened Sectarian Violence Raises Concerns About Civil War

- Hundreds of Iraqis have been killed since the February 22, 2006 bombing of a Shiite mosque in Samarra. [*Associated Press*, 3/23/06]

- The security situation in Iraq is "changing in its nature from insurgency toward sectarian violence," a situation that Abizaid said "is of great concern to all of us." [Testimony of U.S. Central Command Chief General John Abizaid before the Senate Appropriations Committee hearing, 3/9/06; *U.S. News and World Report*, 3/20/06]

- "U.S. Ambassador Zalmay Khalilzad said the 'potential is there' for sectarian violence to become full-blown civil war." [*LA Times*, 3/7/06]

- Former Interim Prime Minister Iyad Allawi told the British Broadcasting Company: "It is unfortunate that we are in civil war," [*LA Times*, 3/20/06]

Political:

- Former Interim Prime Minister Iyad Allawi told the British Broadcasting Company: "It is unfortunate that we are in civil war," [*LA Times*, 3/20/06]

- Despite the fact that national elections were conducted three months ago, there is still no consensus on will run Iraq. Kurds, Sunnis and secular parties have said that they will not support the Shiite majority party's choice of Ibrahim al Jaafari to remain Prime Minister. [*American Forces Press Services*, 3/12/06]

- Several of Iraq's ministries have misused, misspent or simply lost track of billions of dollars. [*Boston Globe*, 2/27/06; *New York Times*, 2/5/06]

- "[E]ven moderate Sunni Arab leaders see violence as a complement to their political platforms and are pursuing a 'dual-track' policy of political engagement and armed resistance." [Testimony of Lieutenant General Michael D. Maples, U.S. Army Director, Defense Intelligence Agency in front of the Senate Armed Services Committee testimony, 2/28/06]

- Many have expressed concern that Iraq's constitution does not adequately ensure the rights of women and religious minorities. [Carnegie Endowment for International Peace, 9/16/05; United States Commission on International Religious Freedom, 10/6/05]

Economic/Reconstruction:

- Many have expressed concern that Iraq's constitution does not adequately ensure the rights of women and religious minorities. [Carnegie Endowment for International Peace, 9/16/05; United States Commission on International Religious Freedom, 10/6/05]

- Unemployment in Iraq is between 25-40 percent. [Brookings Iraq Index, 3/20/06]

- Billions in U.S. taxpayer funds appropriated for the reconstruction of Iraq are either unaccounted for, stolen or have been misspent. [Report of the Special Inspector General for Iraq Reconstruction, January 2006]

- The U.S. is spending 22% of the $18.4 billion appropriated for reconstruction on security, leaving many reconstruction projects incomplete, particularly in critical areas like water, energy and health. [Report of the Special Inspector General for Iraq Reconstruction, January 2006]

- Crude oil production has declined from a pre-war level of 2.5 million barrels-per-day to 1.9 million barrels-per-day. [Brookings Iraq Index, 3/20/06; Department of Defense's (DoD) "Measuring Stability and Security in Iraq" Report, 2/06]

- Electricity production is currently at 4,000 megawatts, compared to 4,500 megawatts before the war. [Report of the Special Inspector General for Iraq Reconstruction, January 2006]

- The international community has only delivered $3.2 billion of the $13.6 billion it pledged in 2003 to help Iraq's reconstruction. [Measuring Stability and Security in Iraq, Department of Defense, 2/06]

Democratic Record on Iraq

Democrats Have Led the Way in Calling for a Change of Course in Iraq.

➤ **As Early as October 2003, Democrats Were Demanding That the President Develop A <u>Plan</u> for Postwar Iraq.** In October 2003, Democrats sought to offer an amendment to the FY 2003 Iraq Supplemental that, among its provisions, would have required President Bush to submit to Congress a <u>plan</u> for postwar Iraq – a coherent and workable strategy to accomplish our mission. It had been clear from the moment that Baghdad fell in April 2003 that our mission in Iraq was being undermined by a lack of planning. Now, more than two years later, Democrats are still insisting that the President develop a coherent plan – but the President continues saying "stay the course." Republicans voted to block consideration of this key Democratic amendment – by a vote of 221 to 202. [*2003 Vote #544*, 10/16/03]

➤ **In June 2005, Democrats Fought to Require the President to Submit A "Strategy for Success" in Iraq.** In June 2005, Democrats sought to offer a key amendment to the FY 2006 DOD Appropriations bill to require the President to submit a "strategy for success" in Iraq, including clear benchmarks for determining when our troops can begin coming home. Our troops have paid a heavy price for this Administration's bungled handling of Iraq. The least this President owes the troops and owes the country is a clear explanation of what the criteria for success in Iraq are and what benchmarks the President will be using in determining when our troops can begin coming home. However, the President has yet to submit this strategy. Republicans voted to block consideration of this amendment – by a vote of 223 to 200. [*2005 House Vote # 269*, 6/16/05]

➤ **In November 2005, Democrats Led the Charge for 2006 to be a Year of Significant Transition in Iraq.** A bipartisan majority of the Senate called for the President to change course in Iraq in order to make 2006 a year of significant transition. Led by Democrats, 79 Senators called on the President to explain to Congress and the American people his strategy for success in Iraq so that our troops can begin to come home. [*RC 323*, S. Amdt. 2518 to S. 1042, 11/15/05, 79-19]

Democrats Have Been Supporting Our Troops in Iraq with Actions.

➤ **Better Pay for the Troops.** Since 2003, Democrats have been consistently fighting for better pay for the troops in Iraq. In 2003, Democrats led the fight to make the increase in imminent danger pay and the family separation allowance <u>permanent</u> – over the opposition of the Bush Administration. This Democratic-led fight was successful in 2004 when these provisions were included in the DOD Authorization bill. In 2003, Democrats also offered an amendment to the Iraqi supplemental that would have provided a $1,500 bonus for troops serving in Iraq and Afghanistan – the Republicans defeated the bonus by a 213 to 213 tie vote. [*2003 House Vote #554*, 10/17/03]

➤ **More Funding for Body Armor and Other Equipment for Our Troops in Iraq.** Every step along the way, Democrats have sought to ensure that our troops were fully equipped for the war in Iraq. For example, because of Democratic efforts, the 2003 Iraqi Supplemental included more funds for body armor. In addition, Democrats offered amendments to shift $322 million from reconstruction to safety equipment for U.S. troops in Iraq (Sen. Dodd) and to shift $3.6 billion from Iraqi reconstruction to support and safety for our troops, including funding for repairing and replacing the critical equipment for combat in Iraq (Rep. Obey). However, both of these efforts were rejected by Republicans. [*RC 376*, S. Amdt. 1817 to S. 1689, Motion to table, 49-37, 10/2/03; H.R. 3289, 2003 House Vote #547, 209-216, 10/16/03]

> **Reimbursing Soldiers and Families for Body Armor.** During the first two and a half years of the war, the Pentagon was sending many of our troops to Iraq without the body armor that they needed. As a result, there were thousands of stories of troops and their family members finding body armor on their own and paying for it out of their own pockets. Although the Pentagon now claims that this problem has been solved, there continue to be stories of troops having to pay for body armor themselves. Democrats have successfully worked to ensure that troops and family members who have been forced to pay for body armor out of their own pockets are reimbursed (Dodd amendment). [S. Amdt. 1970 to *H.R. 2683*, 10/5/05, adopted by voice]

> **More Funding for Up-Armored Humvees.** Democrats have also worked to provide additional funding for up-armored Humvees. For example, on April 21, 2005, Democrats were successful in getting an amendment adopted that would provide an additional $213 million to the Army for the procurement of additional up-armored Humvees. The need for more up-armored Humvees has been well-documented. As Newsweek reported in 2004, "According to an unofficial study by a defense consultant, ... perhaps one in four of those killed in combat in Iraq might be alive if they had had stronger armor around them." [*RC 108*, S.Amdt 52 to *H.R. 1268*, 4/21/05, 61-39; *Newsweek*, 5/3/04]

Democrats Fight Against Waste, Fraud and Abuse in Iraqi Contracting.

> **Democrats Fight for "Truman Committee" to Investigate Waste, Fraud and Abuse in U.S. Contracts in Iraq, including Halliburton Contracts.** The precedent for a select committee to investigate government contracting during wartime is the Truman Select Committee. This committee investigated waste, fraud and abuse in military contracts during World War II. It held 432 public hearings and 300 executive sessions. By the time of its dissolution, its recommendations saved the American taxpayer an estimated $15 billion. A Truman Committee is needed once again. Since 2003, there have been many examples of the misuse of American taxpayer dollars in Iraqi contracting. A key example of Iraqi contract abuses is Halliburton – with Pentagon auditors questioning $1.4 billion of the billings that Halliburton submitted for its Iraqi work. Over the last year, Republicans have rejected the Truman Committee on four separate votes. In addition to Democrats fighting for the Truman Committee, since the beginning of the war in Iraq, the Senate Democratic Policy Committee has held seven oversight hearings on waste, fraud and abuse in Iraqi contracts. [*2005 House Vote #72*, 3/15/05; *2005 House Vote #159*, 5/5/05; *2005 House Vote #297*, 6/22/05; *2006 House Vote #40*, 3/15/06; Senate Democratic Policy Committee hearings, 11/3/03, 2/13/04, 9/10/04, 2/14/05, 6/27/05, 9/16/05, 1/23/06]

> **Democrats Fight to Combat War Profiteering.** Democrats have also been fighting for legislation that would prohibit profiteering by any corporation from any military, relief or reconstruction related efforts in Iraq and attach penalties of up to thirty years in prison for violations. Democrats offered the anti-war profiteering legislation as a motion to recommit in November 2005, but Republicans defeated the motion by a vote of 201 to 221. [*2005 House Vote #584*, 11/9/05; *H.R. 3673* and *S. 1813* in the 108th Congress]

Democrats Urge Bush Administration to Secure More Regional Support in Iraq.

> **Democrats Call for Creation of a Regional Security Group.** Although the Administration has touted short-term conferences on Iraq, these conferences have yielded

few sustainable results. Democrats have urged the Administration to establish a regional security group, whose assistance could go a long way towards stabilizing Iraq. [*Wall Street Journal*, 2/10/05]

Rhetoric vs. Reality on Iraq

Rhetoric: Iraq Has Reconstituted Its Nuclear Weapon Program and Poses An Imminent Threat to the United States. "America must not ignore the threat gathering against us. Facing clear evidence of peril, we cannot wait for the final proof – the smoking gun – that could come in the form of a mushroom cloud. [Saddam Hussein] is moving ever closer to developing a nuclear weapon." [President Bush, Speech in Cincinnati, 10/8/02]

Reality: Iraq Did Not Have Nuclear Weapons. "Saddam Hussein ended the nuclear weapons program in 1991 following the Gulf War. ISG found no evidence to suggest concerted efforts to restart the program." [Iraq Survey Group final report, key findings, 10/6/04]

Rhetoric: Iraq Has Links to Al-Qaeda. "There is no question in my mind about the al Qaeda connection… And the most important thing for Americans and for the entire world to remember is that the potential marriage of weapons of mass destruction with terrorism is everyone's worst nightmare and you have, with Saddam Hussein, both a terrorist link and an insistence on having weapons of mass destruction which he could easily transfer at any time to one of his terrorist associations." [Then National Security Advisor Condoleezza Rice, CNN's Larry King Live, 2/5/03]

Reality: No Evidence of "Operational Relationship" between Iraq and Al-Qaeda. "[A]fter a lengthy investigation, the National Commission on Terrorist Attacks Upon the United States…reported finding no evidence of a 'collaborative operational relationship' between the two or an Iraqi role in attacking the United States." [*Washington Post*, 10/25/04]

Rhetoric: Bush Administration Did Not Manipulate Pre-War Intelligence. "What is not legitimate – and what I will say again is dishonest and reprehensible – is the suggestion by some U.S. senators that the President of the United States or any member of his administration purposely misled the American people on pre-war intelligence." [Vice President Cheney, Remarks on the War on Terror, 11/21/05]

Reality: Former State Department Official Questions the Bush Administration's Use of Pre-War Intelligence. Lawrence Wilkerson, the Former Chief of Staff to Former Secretary of State Colin Powell, said, "[A]fter looking back at it, doing research over the last year or two, and my time in the State Department, there's no doubt in my mind that certain members of the Bush administration did in fact politicize the intelligence." [CNN, 3/17/06]

Critics of the Bush/Republican Iraq Policy

Former National Security Advisor to President George H.W. Bush Brent Scowcroft: "This was said to be part of the war on terror, but Iraq feeds terrorism." [*New Yorker Magazine*, 10/31/05]

Former CENTCOM Commander General Anthony Zinni: "[T]here were a number of people, before we even engaged in this conflict, that felt strongly we were underestimating the problems and the scope of the problems we would have in there. Not just generals, but others—diplomats, those in the international community that understood the situation. Friends of ours in the region that were cautioning us to be careful out there. I think he should have known that." ["60 Minutes," 5/21/04]

The Defense Science Board, the Department of Defense's Own Advisory Think Tank: "'It is clear that Americans who waged the war and who have attempted to mold the aftermath have no clear idea of the framework that has molded the personalities and attitudes of Iraqis.'" [*Washington Post Magazine*, quoting a 2003 report by the Defense Science Board, 11/13/05]

The U.S. National Intelligence Council: Iraq has become "a training and recruitment ground (for terrorists), and an opportunity for terrorists to enhance their technical skills." [*Washington Post*, 1/14/05]

Former Secretary of the Army Thomas White: "We went in with the minimum force to accomplish the military objectives, which was a straightforward task, never really in question…And then we immediately found ourselves shorthanded in the aftermath. We sat there and watched people dismantle and run off with the country, basically." [Quoted in James Fallows, "Blind into Baghdad," *The Atlantic Monthly*, 1/1/04]

Major General Paul Eaton (Ret), who was responsible for training Iraqi troops: "There was no—zero—sense of urgency on the part of the secretary of defense to--to provide the requisite resources to--to truly develop the Iraqi security forces." [CBS News, 3/14/06]

Senior Army Commander General William Wallace: "The plan was based on assumptions that proved not to be true." [CBS News, 3/14/06]

Conservative Icon William F. Buckley: "One can't doubt that the American objective in Iraq has failed." [*National Review*, 2/24/06]

AMENDMENT NO._____   Calendar No._____

Purpose: To clarify and recommend changes to the policy of the United States on Iraq and to require reports on certain matters relating to Iraq.

IN THE SENATE OF THE UNITED STATES—109th Cong., 1st Sess.

S. 1042

AMENDMENT No. 2518

To a~   By...~Warner - Frist~....................tary

....itary

To:........~S 1042~.................~part-

....~ for

....~other

.................~6~.................
Page(s)

GPO: 2000 68–330 (mac)

Referred to the Committee on _____ and ordered to be printed

Ordered to lie on the table and to be printed

AMENDMENT intended to be proposed by ~Mr. LEVIN~ *Mr. Warner, Mr Frist* (for ~himself, Mr. BIDEN, Mr. REID,~ Mr. DODD, Mr. KERRY, ~Mr. FEINGOLD, Mr. DURBIN, Mr. REED, Mr. KENNEDY, and Mrs. FEINSTEIN~)

Viz:

1   At the end of title XII, add the following:

2 **SEC.   . UNITED STATES POLICY ON IRAQ.**

3   (a) SHORT TITLE.—This section may be cited as the

4 "United States Policy on Iraq Act".

1 (b) SENSE OF SENATE.—It is the sense of the Senate

2 that, in order to succeed in Iraq—

3 (1) members of the United States Armed

4 Forces who are serving or have served in Iraq and

5 their families deserve the utmost respect and the

6 heartfelt gratitude of the American people for their

7 unwavering devotion to duty, service to the Nation,

8 and selfless sacrifice under the most difficult cir-

9 cumstances;

10 (2) it is important to recognize that the Iraqi

11 people have made enormous sacrifices and that the

12 overwhelming majority of Iraqis want to live in

13 peace and security;

14 (3) calendar year 2006 should be a period of

15 significant transition to full Iraqi sovereignty, with

16 Iraqi security forces taking the lead for the security

17 of a free and sovereign Iraq, thereby creating the

18 conditions for the phased redeployment of United

19 States forces from Iraq;

20 (4) United States military forces should not

21 stay in Iraq any longer than required ~~indefinitely~~ and the people of Iraq

22 should be so advised;

23 (5) the Administration should tell the leaders of

24 all groups and political parties in Iraq that they

25 need to make the compromises necessary to achieve

1 the broad-based and sustainable political settlement

2 that is essential for defeating the insurgency in Iraq,

3 within the schedule they set for themselves; and

4   (6) the Administration needs to explain to Con-

5 gress and the American people its strategy for the

6 successful completion of the mission in Iraq.

7 (c) REPORTS TO CONGRESS ON UNITED STATES

8 POLICY AND MILITARY OPERATIONS IN IRAQ.—Not later

9 than ~~30~~ 90 days after the date of the enactment of this Act,

10 and every three months thereafter until all United States

11 combat brigades have redeployed from Iraq, the President

12 shall submit to Congress an unclassified report on United

13 States policy and military operations in Iraq. Each report

14 shall include, To the extent practible, the following unclassified information:

15   (1) The current military mission and the diplo-

16 matic, political, economic, and military measures, if

17 any, that are being or have been undertaken to suc-

18 cessfully complete or support that mission, including:

19   (A) Efforts to convince Iraq's main com-

20 munities to make the compromises necessary

21 for a broad-based and sustainable political set-

22 tlement.

23   (B) Engaging the international community

24 and the region in the effort to stabilize Iraq

and to forge a broad-based and sustainable political settlement.

(C) Strengthening the capacity of Iraq's
government ministries.

(D) Accelerating the delivery of basic services.

(E) Securing the delivery of pledged economic assistance from the international community and additional pledges of assistance.

(F) Training Iraqi security forces and
transferring security responsibilities to those
forces and the government of Iraq.

(2) Whether the Iraqis have made the compromises necessary to achieve the broad-based and
sustainable political settlement that is essential for
defeating the insurgency in Iraq.

(3) Any specific conditions included in the April
2005 Multi-National Forces-Iraq campaign action
plan (referred to in United States Government Accountability Office October 2005 report on Rebuild-
ing Iraq: DOD Reports Should Link Economic, Gov-
ernance, and Security Indicators to Conditions for
Stabilizing Iraq), and any subsequent updates to
that campaign plan, that must be met in order to

1 provide for the transition of security responsibility to

2 Iraqi security forces.

3 (4) To the extent that these conditions are not

4 covered under paragraph (3), the following should

5 also be addressed:

6 (A) The number of battalions of the Iraqi

7 Armed Forces that must be able to operate

8 independently or to take the lead in

9 counterinsurgency operations and the defense of

10 Iraq's territory.

11 (B) The number of Iraqi special police

12 units that must be able to operate independ-

13 ently or to take the lead in maintaining law and

14 order and fighting the insurgency.

15 (C) The number of regular police that

16 must be trained and equipped to maintain law

17 and order.

18 (D) The ability of Iraq's Federal ministries

19 and provincial and local governments to inde-

20 pendently sustain, direct, and coordinate Iraq's

21 security forces.

22 (5) The criteria to be used to evaluate progress

23 toward meeting such conditions.

24 (6) A schedule for meeting such conditions, an

25 assessment of the extent to which such conditions

1   have been met, information regarding variables that

2   could alter that schedule, and the reasons for any

3   subsequent changes to that schedule.

Progress in Iraq

2006 First Quarter
Report Card

Progress in Iraq:
2006 First Quarter Report Card

Subject	Grade
Overall First Quarter Grade:	D
Security and Stability	D-
Governance and Democracy:	C+
Economic Reconstruction:	D-
Impact on U.S. National Security:	F

First Quarter Report Card

In the first three months of 2006, the Bush administration has failed to achieve substantial progress on the security and reconstruction of Iraq, even though there have been some achievements in forming a democratic government. Thousands of U.S. soldiers and diplomats continue to serve their country bravely but they remain tied to the stay-the-course policies of President Bush and his top policy and political leadership. Judging the administration's Iraq policy as a whole, the Center for American Progress gives the Bush administration a "D" for its performance in the first quarter of 2006.

This report follows last year's vote by a bipartisan majority of 79 Senators which called on President Bush to put forward a strategy for "the successful completion of the mission in Iraq" and declared 2006 "to be a period of significant transition for Iraq." This vote of no-confidence in the Bush administration's Iraq policy prompted President Bush to mount a two-month public relations offensive, a campaign that left many unanswered questions. This report seeks to fill the gaps left unmet by the Bush administration's incomplete status reports on Iraq.

Overall First Quarter Grade	**D**
Security and Stability	**D-**
Governance and Democracy	**C+**
Economic Reconstruction	**D-**
Impact on U.S. National Security	**F**

Overall First Quarter Grade   D

Security and Stability   D-

- U.S. efforts to train Iraqi security forces have achieved some tangible results, with more Iraqi forces in the lead of key operations. This progress increases chances for a much-needed redeployment of U.S. troops.

- Sectarian violence sparked by last month's bombing of a Shiite shrine in Samarra brought Iraq to the brink of all-out civil war.

Governance and Democracy   C+

- U.S. Ambassador to Iraq Zalmay Khalilzad has played a constructive role in attempting to broker a political agreement among Iraqi political factions. This diplomatic work is vital to stabilizing Iraq. Three months after Iraq's elections, the new parliament convened for the first time.

- Three months after the December elections, divisions among Iraqi political leaders run the risk of preventing them from meeting the deadline to form a new government.

Economic Reconstruction   D-

- After spending months promoting its provincial reconstruction teams (PRTs), this key component of the Bush administration main reconstruction plan is still mostly dormant.

- Iraq produces less oil now than it did on the eve of the invasion, and many Iraqis continue to suffer from a lack of basic services.

Impact on U.S. National Security   F

- Three years of a continuous U.S. troop presence in Iraq has weakened U.S. ground forces.

- The open-ended commitment to Iraq has served as a rallying cry for global terrorists.

- U.S. intelligence agencies have warned that Iraq has become the new leading training ground for global terrorists

- The total costs of the war continue to rise, approaching $300 billion for American taxpayers, including the forthcoming bill for supplemental funding.

Security and Stability: D-

In the first quarter of 2006, Iraq continued to suffer from instability and sectarian violence. This was due in part to internal disturbances but also due to the continuing effects of past U.S. decisions such as sending in too few troops after the invasion[1] and failing to disband the militias.[2]

1. **Increased threat of all-out civil war.** A series of brutal attacks sparked by the February 22 bombing of the holy Shiite Al-Askari shrine in Samarra raised fears that a nightmare scenario might become a reality: Iraq descending into a full-blown sectarian civil war that could draw its neighboring countries into the conflict. Hundreds of Iraqis have since been killed in score-settling violence.

2. **Growing evidence of death squads connected to the Iraqi ministries.** In the first quarter, there were several incidents involving "death squads" with alleged ties to the Ministry of Interior.

3. **Mixed results in training the Iraqi army.** The Bush administration reported that it had trained and equipped nearly 250,000 Iraqi security forces by mid-March. Though the Iraqi security forces have not met expectations, the Iraqi Army saw overall improvement in the first quarter of 2006. If this training continues on pace, it could open the door for substantial U.S. troop redeployments in 2006.

   - **Overall increased readiness.** Ninety-eight Iraqi army battalions are now combat ready, ten more than reported three months ago. There has been a 47 percent increase in battalions classified as "in the lead" (to 53 today from 36 in October 2005). Iraqi security forces took the lead in maintaining a relative calm during the December elections and October referendum last year, and Iraqi security forces were at the forefront of enforcing the recent curfews that temporarily stemmed recent violence.

   - **No independent battalions.** The Pentagon reported in February that the number of Iraqi army battalions judged capable of fighting the insurgency without U.S. help slipped from one to zero.

---

[1] The Bush administration decided to enter Iraq with fewer troops than the Army chief of staff recommended was needed for stability operations. The Administration acted on a belief that Iraqis would rapidly create their own inclusive government, thus allowing the United States to withdraw troops in a matter of weeks after toppling Saddam Hussein. This created a vacuum and gave space for terrorist groups to fan the flames of sectarian and ethnic tensions.

[2] The Bush administration failed to implement its own Coalition Provisional Authority's June 2004 order to disband the militias that are a key challenge in Iraq, allowing these groups to grow and increase their control of territory. As a result, ethnic and sectarian militias control large sections of the country, without a strong allegiance to a unified Iraqi government. In addition to an estimated 100,000 Kurdish Peshmerga forces, numerous Shiite militias exist, including the Mahdi Army, which killed U.S. forces in 2004.

4. **Unfinished work with Iraqi ministries impedes security transition.** A key factor that prevents Iraqi Army units from making the transition from being "in the lead" (Level 2) to "independent" (Level 1) is the unfinished work in the institutional development of the Ministries of Defense and Interior. These ministries have not yet developed the necessary budgeting, contracting, personnel management, and logistical procedures.

5. **Corruption, absenteeism, and militia infiltration of Iraqi police.** According to the Bush administration, a total of 127,700 Iraqi police and other forces under the Ministry of Interior have received training and equipment. But infiltration by militias, ongoing corruption, and absenteeism remain major problems. Iraqi investigators recently broke up a kidnapping and extortion ring in northern Baghdad, which was commanded by a general in the Iraqi police. Iraqi and U.S. officials have begun to address these problems but much work remains undone.

Governance and Democracy: C+

U.S. Ambassador Zalmay Khalilzad's active intervention in the formation of a new Iraqi government has helped push the parties closer together. But underlying ethnic and sectarian tensions remain and human rights abuses continue.

1. **New parliament convenes, political negotiations continue.** Iraq's new parliament convened briefly on March 16, and negotiations among the main political groups on forming a new government continue, with constructive intervention from U.S. ambassador Zalmay Khalilzad. This intervention has helped stabilize a tenuous situation.

2. **December 2005 election reveals growing sectarian divisions.** As the Bush administration's status reports indicate, turnout for Iraq's elections increased to 77 percent in the December 2005 elections, up from 58 percent in the January 2005 elections. The December election results, however, revealed growing divisions in the country. The vast majority of Iraqis voted for ethnic or sectarian based parties, and national unity tickets garnered slim support.

3. **Human rights abuses and civil liberties infringements continue.** Despite two elections and a referendum, the country remains in the very early and fragile stages of a long-term process of building a real democracy. Released in the first quarter, the Bush administration's State Department report on human rights in Iraq notes widespread problems, including a "pervasive climate of violence, misappropriation of official authority by sectarian, criminal, terrorist, and insurgent groups," and "arbitrary deprivation of life," among other problems. Iraqis do not live in freedom, according to Freedom House, which has provided the gold standard for measuring trends in political rights and civil liberties over the past three decades. Freedom House warned that the new constitution "could threaten human rights" by allowing possible restrictions on the rights of women, religious minorities, and democratic and legitimate political opposition.

Economic Reconstruction Track: D-

The Bush administration has failed to implement its primary reconstruction program and has been forced to divert billions of dollars meant to provide basic services to Iraqis. Oil production has fallen below pre-war output and electricity production continues to be sporadic.

1. **Bush administration has not fully implemented plans.** After spending months promoting its provincial reconstruction teams (PRTs), the Bush administration main plan for reconstruction is "still mostly dormant." Only three of 16 planned teams have been launched. Stuart Bowen, the U.S. Special Inspector for Iraq and a former counsel in the Bush White House, reported earlier this year that the United States failed to keep track of at least $9 billion and did not exercise adequate managerial controls over the money. The United States has also been forced to divert to security $3 billion, which has derailed basic water and electricity projects.

2. **Oil production still stuck at prewar levels.** In the first quarter, Iraq's oil production remains stuck at prewar levels, averaging under 2 million barrels per day. Prewar oil production was 2.5 million barrels per day.

3. **Advances in electricity production, but still not meeting overall demand.** The State Department reports an increase in overall electricity output of 17 percent in March 2006 (compared to the March 2006), but on average Iraqis only receive electricity about half of the day. Residents of Baghdad receive 7 hours of electricity a day on average.

4. **Double digit unemployment**. Best estimates of unemployment in Iraq range from 25 to 40 percent.

Impact on U.S. National Security: F

1. **Impact on U.S. Military**

   - **Casualties of war.** As of March 16, 2006, 2,310 U.S. troops have lost their lives in Operation Iraqi Freedom and 17,124 have been wounded in action. This includes 134 troops killed and 835 wounded from January 1 to March 16 this year. One in five veterans in Iraq shows evidence of mental health problems according to a recent study in the *Journal of the American Medical Association*. More than a third of U.S. soldiers and Marines fighting in Iraq visited a mental health specialist at least once after their combat tour.

   - **U.S. ground forces stretched thin.** Three years of a continuous U.S. troop presence in Iraq has weakened U.S. ground forces. Several recent studies highlight that extended deployments in Iraq have eroded U.S. ground forces and overall military strength, including a Pentagon-commissioned study that concluded that the Army cannot maintain its current pace of operations in Iraq without leaving permanent damage. Almost all available combat units in the U.S. Army, including units in the National Guard and Reserve have been deployed to Iraq at least once. Some are returning for second and third tours.

- **Recruitment shortfalls as a result of Iraq**. The Army met its recruiting goals in fiscal year 2006 but only by significantly lowering its goals for the first part of the fiscal year. In 2005, the active-duty Army missed its annual recruiting goal by 6,627 soldiers. This shortfall was the largest in two decades, occurring despite the fact that the Army added 1,300 recruiters, sharply increased its recruiting budget, offered huge bonuses and lowered standards.

- **Decline in recruitment standards.** In FY 2005, the Army took its least qualified recruits in a decade as measured by educational and test results. The percentage of new recruits in the Army without a high school diploma rose to 13 percent in 2005, up from 8 percent in 2004. The Army has also dramatically increased the number of recruits who previously would have been barred from military service because of criminal misconduct or drug and alcohol problems.

2. Impact on the War on Terrorism

- **Iraq serving as a rallying cry for global terrorists**. By maintaining an open-ended military presence in Iraq, the Bush administration continues to give global terrorist groups a potent recruitment tool. In the first quarter of 2006, there have been 620 incidents of terrorism in the world, up from 415 terrorist incidents in the first quarter of 2003.

- **Iraq serving as live exercise training ground for global terrorists.** By invading Iraq without a plan to stabilize the country, the Bush administration created a new terrorist haven where none had previously existed. The Central Intelligence Agency's National Intelligence Council warned last year that Iraq has become the new leading training ground for global terrorists. In the first quarter of this year, U.S. intelligence and military officials voiced concerns that terrorists were taking their newly acquired skills in Iraq and using them in Afghanistan, where the battle against terrorists remains incomplete.

3. Financial Costs of the War

- **Straining the U.S. budget.** The total costs of the war continue to rise, approaching $300 billion for American taxpayers, including the forthcoming bill for supplemental funding. The Congressional Budget Office estimates that in their mid-range scenario, the Iraq war will cost approximately $266 billion in the next decade, making the direct cost of the Iraq war around $500 billion.

- **Leading to long-term financial costs.** A study by two academic experts, Harvard budget expert Linda Bilmes and Columbia University Professor and Nobel Laureate Joseph E. Stiglitz, estimate that the war could cost the United States a minimum of nearly one trillion dollars and potentially over two trillion dollars. They include costs such as lifetime disability and health care for the injured, the economic value of lives lost, and the war's related effects on investment, oil prices, and the growing US budget deficit.

5. **Higher oil prices.** In March 2005, global oil prices averaged around $56 a barrel, nearly double what they were on the eve of the Iraq war in 2003 ($30 a barrel). Though some of the increases reflect rising demand in Asia, oil market analysts have noted that the decline in Iraq's production as well as a risk premium resulting from increased insecurity in the Middle East has contributed to higher prices.

Progress in Iraq:
2006 First Quarter Report Card

Subject	Grade
Overall First Quarter Grade:	D
Security and Stability	D-
Governance and Democracy:	C+
Economic Reconstruction:	D-
Impact on U.S. National Security:	F

Real Security:
Protecting America and Restoring Our Leadership in the World

IRAQ: Additional Resources

Bush Administration Claims, Intelligence and Failures:

***The Bush Administration's Public Statements on Iraq: Iraq on the Record*, House Governmental Reform Committee, Minority Office.** "Iraq on the Record is a searchable collection of 237 specific misleading statements made by Bush Administration officials about the threat posed by Iraq. It contains statements that were misleading based on what was known to the Administration at the time the statements were made." [Available at: http://democrats.reform.house.gov/IraqOnTheRecord/]

***WMD in Iraq: Evidence and Implications*, Carnegie Endowment for International Peace, January 2004.** This study "details what the U.S. and international intelligence communities understood about Iraq's weapons programs before the war and outlines policy reforms to improve threat assessments, deter transfer of WMD to terrorists, strengthen the U.N. weapons inspection process, and avoid politicization of the intelligence process." [Available at: http://www.carnegieendowment.org/publications/index.cfm?fa=view&id=1435]

"Blueprint for a Mess," *New York Times Magazine*, **11/2/03.** Documents six major mistakes made by the Bush Administration and how they affected the situation in Iraq: (1) Getting in too deep with Chalabi; (2) Shutting out the State Department; (3) too little planning too late; (4) The Troops: Too Few, Too Constricted; (5) Neglecting the Office of Reconstruction and Humanitarian Assistance; and (6) Ignoring the Shiites.

***Intelligence, Policy, and the War in Iraq* by Paul R. Pillar,** *Foreign Affairs*, **March/April 2006.** The intelligence community's former senior analyst for the Middle East writes that the Bush Administration "disregarded the community's expertise, politicized the intelligence process, and selected unrepresentative raw intelligence to make its public case."

"Why Iraq Has No Army," *The Atlantic Monthly*, **December 2005.** This article chronicles why the development of a viable Iraqi security force has taken so long.

Current situation in Iraq:

Brookings Iraq Index. A statistical compilation of economic, public opinion, and security data. Updated every Monday and Thursday. [Available at: http://www.brookings.org/iraqindex]

Reports of the Special Inspector General for Iraq Reconstruction. [Available at: http://www.sigir.mil/]

The Next Iraqi War? Sectarianism and Civil Conflict, **International Crisis Group, 2/27/06.** This report warns that "Iraq is teetering on the threshold of wholesale disaster…Iraqi political actors and the international community must act urgently to prevent a low-intensity conflict from escalating into an all-out civil war that could lead to Iraq's disintegration and destabilize the entire region." [Available at: http://www.crisisgroup.org/home/index.cfm?id=3980&l=1]

The **U.S. Commission on Religious Freedom** and the non-partisan **Freedom House** have good resources about human rights and religious freedom in Iraq. You can find these resources at: http://www.uscirf.gov/ and http://www.freedomhouse.org/

New Strategies for Iraq

A Switch in Time: A New Strategy for America in Iraq, **Kenneth M. Pollack and the Iraq Policy Working Group of the Saban Center for Middle East Policy at the Brookings Institution.** This report "details a comprehensive, alternative approach to current U.S. military, political, and economic policies in Iraq." [Available here: http://www.brookings.org/fp/saban/analysis/20060215_iraqreport.pdf]

Strategic Redeployment, **Center for American Progress, 9/29/05.** A Progressive Plan for Iraq and the Struggle Against Violent Extremists. [Available at: http://www.americanprogress.org/]

SERVICE MEMBERS IN IRAQ & AFGHANISTAN, BY STATE

STATE	Currently Deployed, as of January 2006	Deployed Since Beginning of War, 2003
Alabama	3,550	22,440
Alaska	6,020	20,539
Arizona	3,568	18,752
Arkansas	1,744	12,811
California	18,879	109,721
Colorado	3,073	14,311
Connecticut	1,285	8,891
Delaware	428	3,350
DC	202	1,182
Florida	21,897	126,713
Georgia	7,862	32,973
Hawaii	868	6,273
Idaho	1,122	7,994
Illinois	8,515	46,244
Indiana	4,061	19,380
Iowa	2,079	11,610
Kansas	2,340	11,318
Kentucky	2,313	11,805
Louisiana	2,824	21,609
Maine	936	5,712
Maryland	2,948	16,780
Massachusetts	2,264	13,503
Michigan	6,527	35,409
Minnesota	2,142	13,542
Mississippi	2,224	16,293
Missouri	4,976	24,026
Montana	1,456	8,101
Nebraska	1,532	7,990
Nevada	1,903	11,016
New Hampshire	1,187	7,292
New Jersey	3,544	29,742
New Mexico	1,681	8,332
New York	9,116	48,672
North Carolina	5,815	30,107
North Dakota	538	3,792
Ohio	6,569	39,309
Oklahoma	2,431	15,494
Oregon	2,459	15,611
Pennsylvania	9,423	50,609
Rhode Island	678	3,536
South Carolina	3,283	19,418
South Dakota	1,105	8,075
Tennessee	8,717	37,892
Texas	31,163	157,185
Utah	1,739	8,543
Vermont	776	3,521
Virginia	5,589	30,551
Washington	6,457	38,219
West Virginia	1,712	11,290
Wisconsin	4,061	17,223
Wyoming	795	4,502
Total	**228,376**	**1,249,203**

SOURCE: Department of Defense Legal Residence/ Home of Record for Service Members Deployed.

ENERGY INDEPENDENCE

Dependence on foreign sources of energy compromises our national security and makes families and businesses less secure because of high, spiking energy costs. Unfortunately, during the Bush Administration, the nation's foreign energy dependence and energy costs have grown, making all Americans less secure and hitting the bottom lines of families and businesses across the country, particularly the airline, trucking, agriculture, and manufacturing sectors. Rather than taking swift action to reduce our dependence and lower prices, the Bush Administration has stood idly by as our overreliance, energy prices and oil company profits reach unprecedented levels. The Administration's energy policy has left the nation vulnerable and does little to prepare for a safer future.

Independence from foreign energy sources will create American jobs and technology, boost competitiveness and improve our national and economic security. American families and businesses send hundreds of billions of dollars every year to foreign oil-producers, many of whom are located in nations that manipulate world energy markets and have potentially unstable forms of government. Investing that money here in America would not only make America more secure by ensuring we have sufficient and affordable sources of energy under our control, but also favorably impact our balance of trade, job creation, and the American economy.

To Free America from Dependence on Foreign Oil, Democrats will:

- Achieve energy independence for America by 2020 by eliminating reliance on oil from the Middle East and other unstable regions of the world.

- Increase production of alternate fuels from America's heartland including bio-fuels, geothermal, clean coal, fuel cells, solar and wind; promote hybrid and flex fuel vehicle technology and manufacturing; enhance energy efficiency and conservation incentives.

Bush/Republican Record on Energy Security

Reliance on and costs of imported energy have increased

U.S. oil and petroleum product imports are increasing. In 2000, the year before President Bush took office, America imported 3.8 billion barrels of oil and petroleum products or 52.9 percent of its total net consumption. In 2005, the U.S. imported about 4.7 billion barrels or 60 percent of its total net consumption. If current policies continue, the Administration projects that Americans will import 5.25 billion barrels in 2020. [Energy Information Administration, *U.S. Imports by Country of Origin*, and *Annual Energy Outlook 2006*]

Americans are spending more on imported oil. In 2000, when oil prices were high relative to the 1990's, Americans sent $109 billion to other countries to purchase crude oil and petroleum products. In 2005, Americans spent nearly 115 percent more money, $232 billion, to purchase these products from foreign countries. [Energy Information Administration, *Annual Energy Review* 2004 and *Annual Energy Outlook 2006*]

The United States is heavily dependent on oil from unstable regions. In 2005, the U.S. imported almost 840 million barrels of oil from the Persian Gulf countries of Bahrain, Iraq, Iran, Kuwait, Qatar, Saudi Arabia, and United Arab Emirates—17 percent of US oil imports. We depend upon the unstable Persian Gulf region to provide 11 percent of all crude oil and petroleum products used in the U.S. In 2005, 41 percent of our oil imports came from the OPEC cartel countries of Algeria, Indonesia, Iraq, Kuwait, Libya, Nigeria, Qatar, Saudi Arabia, United Arab Emirates, and Venezuela. [Energy Information Administration, *US Imports by Country of Origin, February 2006 Petroleum Supply Monthly With Data for December 2005*]

Insecurity for families has grown, as oil profits have skyrocketed

Heating costs have skyrocketed. The average U.S. household will spend about $107 more for heating this winter compared to last year. Households heating with natural gas paid $402, or 86 percent more, to heat their homes this winter than they paid in 2001-2002. Consumers of heating oil paid $759, or 121 percent more, this winter than they paid in 2001-2002. [Energy Information Administration *Short Term Energy Outlook, 3/2006*]

Transportation costs for families have increased by $1,440. Prices at the gas pump have jumped 62.5 percent from $1.44 per gallon in January 2001 to $2.34 in March 2006, while the price for a barrel of oil has more than doubled from $29.26 in January 2001 to $62.16 in February 2006. The average household with children will spend about $3,343 on transportation fuel costs this year, an increase of 75 percent over 2001 costs. [Energy Information Administration, *Retail Gasoline Prices, This Week in Petroleum,* and *Household Vehicle Energy Use: Latest Data and Trends 11/2005*]

Oil companies are raking in extraordinary profits. In 2005, as Americans struggled to pay their gasoline and heating bills, the top six oil companies made an astonishing $113 billion in profits. ExxonMobil reported the highest annual profits in U.S. history; the oil giant's 2005 profits soared to $36.13 billion, an increase of 43 percent over 2004. The oil companies attempt to downplay their profits to the public. However, ExxonMobil's 2004 annual report emphasizes "return on average capital employed" as the best measure for financial performance and reveals a rate of return of 37 percent for domestic drilling and 28.6 percent for domestic refining. [ExxonMobil press release for January 30, 2006; "High Oil Prices Help Boost Exxon Profits," Steve Quinn, AP Business Writer, January 30, 2006; Public Citizen testimony, Senate Judiciary Committee, February 1, 2006]

Farmers spending more on energy. In 2002, farmers spent $18.36 billion on energy for crop production. Increasing prices of natural gas, diesel, and gasoline raised those costs to approximately $46.4 billion in 2004. Even during a good year, farmers operate on profit margins of only about 5 percent. Price increases of 20 percent or more on essential items like fertilizer, fuel, and pesticides have made it very difficult for farmers to get by. [Congressional Research Service report, 11/19/2004]

Insecurity for the American economy has grown

High energy prices are hurting our economy. Energy-intensive industries like manufacturing are struggling with increasing energy costs. High oil and natural gas prices contributed to a record trade deficit at the end of 2005. Economists have estimated that on average, every time oil prices go up 10 percent, 150,000 Americans lose their jobs. [Alan Carruth, Mark Hooker, and Andrew Oswald, "Unemployment Equilibria and Input Prices: Theory and Evidence from the United States," *The Review of Economics and Statistics*, v. 80, n. 4, 1998, p. 621.]

The Bush FY2007 budget makes matters worse. The Bush budget proposes to eliminate research and development funding for geothermal and hydropower energy, building codes assistance, and several new programs the President had originally touted from the *Energy Policy Act of 2005* (EPACT). The budget also contains funding proposals well below authorized levels for clean coal technology, electricity reliability, energy efficiency, energy management within the federal government, weatherization assistance, and energy cost assistance for low-income Americans.

- **President's budget does not match the rhetoric of the State of the Union.** The Bush Administration has cut funding renewable energy for years, and the budget fails to turn this around. His proposed budget increase for clean energy research barely brings these programs back up to approximately 2001 total levels, while Americans paid 50 percent more for energy than in 2001 and energy expenditures are higher as a share of GDP than at any time in the last 18 years. The President's budget also provides 46 percent less than the level promised in the new energy law for renewable energy research. [Senate Energy and Natural Resources, 2/6/06]

- **Cuts renewable energy programs, which create jobs and reduce our dependency on foreign oil.** The President's budget eliminates all funding for bioenergy incentives that help expand the production of ethanol and biodiesel. Further, the budget cuts renewable energy loans (from $177 million to $35 million) and grants, as well as biomass research and development. His budget proposals have been called "pitiful. The $150 million the White House said it would commit to making biofuels more competitive…turns out to be $50 million less than the amount authorized by last year's energy bill." [New York Times, 2/6/06]

- **Slashes energy efficiency and conservation.** The President's budget cuts energy efficiency by 13 percent from last year, even though DOE research on core efficiency programs has been cut by 32 percent in real terms since FY 2002. [Union of Concerned Scientists; American Council for an Energy Efficient Economy, 2/7/05] Reducing our nation's energy consumption is effective in reducing our reliance on foreign energy, but the President's budget cuts conservation programs by $113 million. [House Appropriations Committee, Democratic Staff, 2/6/06]

No energy security solutions from Republicans

Smokescreen solutions to energy problems. Rather than enact policies that would aggressively confront our security challenges and provide safe, sustainable and affordable energy, Republicans have pushed for drilling in the Alaska wilderness and rolling back environmental protections regulating oil and gas leases and refineries. Drilling in the Alaska National Wildlife Refuge would provide only the equivalent of six months of American oil demand and would not provide any oil for a decade, lower prices, or create a significant number of new long-term jobs. Refiners have not shown interest in building new refineries regardless of environmental regulations.

Republicans rejected key measures to increase energy security. During consideration of the energy bill, Republicans rejected Democratic proposals to implement a national renewable portfolio standard, eliminate 40 percent of oil imports by 2020, extend the production tax credit beyond 2008, and confront climate change. Republicans also opposed Democrats' efforts to make room in the FY 2007 budget to fully fund the energy efficiency, vehicle technology and biomass/biofuels programs.

Democratic Record on Energy Security

Democrats want to make America energy independent by 2020 by improving energy security, generating jobs and economic growth, and protecting Americans from price spikes and price gouging. Democrats have proposed to enhance our energy security and achieve energy independence through measures that increase domestic supplies of alternative energy, improve our energy efficiency, and protect consumers.

Making America energy independent

Funding energy research. Democrats support increasing energy research and development funding and extending the renewable energy production tax credit [S. Amdt. 3039]. Democrats proposed $250 million for increasing research, development, demonstration and deployment of new energy generation and new energy efficiency technologies to most effectively support the objective of decreasing U.S. oil imports, which is a critical national security priority. But Republicans blocked consideration of this critical proposal. [*H.R. 2419*, 2005 House Vote #203. Blocked 219-190. 5/24/2005]

Increasing energy efficiency standards and investing in new technology. Democrats sought to provide tax incentives for renewable energy, such as solar, wind, geothermal and biomass, and for energy efficient home appliances and to expand the deployment of the latest technologies and increase research and commercialization of emerging technologies. [*H.R. 6, 2005 House Vote #188.* Rejected 170-259. 4/20/2005]

Creating the next generation of revolutionary energy technologies. Democrats are committed to creating a new DARPA-like initiative to provide seed money for fundamental research needed to develop high-risk, high-reward technologies and build markets for the next generation of revolutionary energy technologies, such as those emerging from biotechnology, nanotechnology, solar, and fuel-cell research. This new agency would have resources and flexibility needed to do ground-breaking research and push promising technology into the marketplace. [*H.R. 4435*, S. 2196]

Expanding biofuels and other clean energy alternatives. Growth in use of biofuels could save 3.9 million barrels of oil per day by 2025. Democrats support tax incentives and a national renewable fuels standard to encourage increased production of renewable fuels. [S. 1994] Democrats have proposed to rapidly expand production and distribution of synthetic and bio-based fuels, such as ethanol derived from cellulosic sources, and deploy new engine technologies for fuel-flexible, hybrid, plug-in hybrid and bio-diesel vehicles -- by doubling research and development funding for new fuels, innovative refining processes for these fuels, and new vehicle technologies so that these emerging technologies can be deployed in the next three to five years. [House Democratic Innovation Agenda, November 2005]

Cutting dependence on foreign oil. Democrats support reducing imports of foreign oil by 40 percent by 2025. [S. Amdt. 784; H. Amdt. 79 to *H.R. 6* is similar]

Creating a tire fuel efficiency program. Proper inflation of tires and replacing old tires with fuel-efficient tires could save 470,000 barrels of oil per day by 2013. Democrats propose creating a national tire fuel efficiency program. [*S. 1882*]

Creating a strategic gasoline and jet fuel reserve. A gasoline and jet fuel reserve, like our Strategic Petroleum Reserve, would protect Americans from price spikes like those Americans experienced after Hurricanes Katrina and Rita. [*S. 1794*]

Enacting a national renewable electricity standard. A national Renewable Portfolio Standard (RPS) would require electric utilities to produce 10 percent of their electricity from renewable sources by 2020. An RPS would reduce our dependence on foreign energy sources and create jobs. [S. Amdt. 791]

Protecting consumers today from price gouging

Banning gasoline price gouging and improving market transparency. Democrats have proposed federal legislation establishing a federal ban on price gouging for oil, gasoline, and other petroleum products during national emergencies, provide civil and criminal penalties for price gouging, ban market manipulation, and require greater transparency in oil and gasoline markets. [*S. 1735, H.R. 3936, S. 1744*, S. Amdt. 2612]

Investigating post-hurricane price gouging. Democrats passed a provision requiring the Federal Trade Commission (FTC) to investigate nationwide gas price spikes in the aftermath of Hurricane Katrina for evidence of price gouging and its effects on the U.S. economy. [S. Amdt. 1703]

Democrats fought to impose tough criminal penalties on price gouging companies. But Republicans voted against new criminal penalties of up to $100 million on price gouging energy corporations. [*2005 House Vote #500, H.R. 3402*, 9/28/05. Motion rejected 195-226: Republicans 0-226; Democrats 194-0)

Senator **Mikulski** and 31 Democratic Senators sent a letter to the President on October 7, 2005 urging him to bring the oil companies' CEOs to the White House and demand that they lower their prices.

Senators **Feingold, Feinstein,** and 13 additional Democratic Senators sent a letter to the Chairwoman of the Federal Trade Commission (FTC) on September 30, 2005 requesting an explanation for the FTC's approval of refinery mergers, which have harmed consumers.

Easing energy prices for consumers

Energy consumer relief for families, small businesses and farmers. Democrats propose to provide relief to families paying skyrocketing energy costs by expanding the Low-Income Home Energy Assistance Program (LIHEAP) and provide relief to small businesses and farmers with a tax credit and grants. These would be paid for by repealing at least $8 billion in unnecessary subsidies in the new energy law for oil and gas companies, which oil companies say they do not even need, and through fines from price-gouging companies. [*H.R. 4479*]

Aiding low-income families with high energy costs. Democrats support full funding of $5.1 billion for the Low-Income Home Energy Assistance Program (LIHEAP) to account for the dramatic increases in cost of heating. LIHEAP budget requests have decreased since 2001 despite 78 percent increases in expenditures on heating fuels. [S. Amdt. 2033, S. Amdt. 2077, S. Amdt. 2194, and S. Amdt. 3074]

Weatherization assistance. Weatherizing homes that use home heating oil could save consumers 18 percent of their heating costs and save 80,000 barrels of oil per day. Democrats support increased funding of the Weatherization Assistance Program, which helps American consumers weatherize their homes, lowering energy consumption and costs. [S. Amdt. 3039]

Rhetoric v. Reality on Energy Security

In his January 2006 State of the Union address, President Bush stated, "America is addicted to oil," and announced an "Advanced Energy Initiative." The President has often promised to make America less dependent on foreign energy by delivering reliable, affordable energy developed with new technology. The President's budget requests, including the President's budget for Fiscal Year 2007, have rarely followed through on the Administration's relatively minor commitments to cleaner, more reliable and affordable energy.

On importing energy

Rhetoric: "Keeping America competitive requires affordable energy. And here we have a serious problem: America is addicted to oil, which is often imported from unstable parts of the world. The best way to break this addiction is through technology." [President Bush, State of the Union Address, 1/31/ 2006]

Reality: The Bush Administration has done very little to address our "oil addiction." In fact, Energy Secretary Bodman has already retracted the President's pledge to reduce imports of Middle Eastern oil, calling it "purely an example." [Press Briefing, 2/1/2006]

On technology

Rhetoric: "So tonight, I announce the Advanced Energy Initiative -- a 22-percent increase in clean-energy research." [President Bush, State of the Union Address, 1/31/ 2006]

Reality: In his Fiscal Year 2007 budget request, the President is proposing to spend less on energy efficiency, conservation, and renewable energy resources in inflation-adjusted dollars than was appropriated in Fiscal Year 2001. DOE energy efficiency and conservation programs would be cut by $21 million.

On conservation

Rhetoric: "We need to do everything we can to improve conservation because there are significant savings to be derived there, as well. And we've done that over the years." [Vice President Cheney, 9/13/2004]

Reality: The federal government is the largest single consumer of energy in the United States. The President's Fiscal Year 2007 request for the Federal Energy Management Program, which improves efficiency in the federal government's use of energy, is nearly the lowest request ever even though the federal government's energy consumption in 2004 was higher than it has been at any time during the last ten years.

Real Security:
Protecting America and Restoring Our Leadership in the World

Energy Independence: Additional Resources

***Winning the Oil Endgame: Innovation for Profits, Jobs, and Security,* Rocky Mountain Institute.** This report offers solutions to reducing dependence on oil through efficiency and technology improvements. [Available at www.oilendgame.com.]

***The Changing Risks in Global Oil Supply and Demand: Crisis or Evolving Solutions,* Center for Strategic and International Studies.** This report details the current and future risks of oil dependence in the global market. [Available at http://www.csis.org/component/option,com_csis_pubs/task,view/id,1855/.]

***Reducing Oil Use Through Energy Efficiency: Opportunties Beyond Cars and Trucks,* American Council for an Energy-Efficient Economy, January 2006.** This report outlines methods of improving the efficiency of American energy use. [Available at http://www.aceee.org/pubs/e061.htm.]

***Testimony before the House Science Committee,* R. James Woolsey, November 1, 2001.** Former CIA Director and longtime public servant James Woolsey details the new energy security risks in America after the September 11 terrorist attacks. [Available at http://www.house.gov/science/hearings/index.htm.]

***How Innovative Technologies, Business Strategies, and Policies Can Dramatically Enhance Energy Security and Prosperity,* Amory Lovins testimony before Senate Energy and Natural Resources Committee, March 7, 2006.** This testimony discusses policy proposals to achieve energy security through energy independence. [Available at http://www.rmi.org/images/other/Energy/E06-02_SenateTestimonial.pdf.]

***Testimony before the Senate Energy and Natural Resources Committee,* R. James Woolsey, March 7, 2006.** Director Woolsey's testimony discusses energy security and its close association with American dependence on petroleum. [Available at http://energy.senate.gov/public/index.cfm?FuseAction=Hearings.Testimony&Hearing_ID=1534&Witness_ID=4342.]

***Testimony before the Senate Energy and Natural Resources Committee,* Frank Verrastro, Center for Strategic and International Studies, March 7, 2006.** Mr. Verrastro's testimony discusses the changing nature of global energy markets and offers policies to increase energy security. [Available at http://energy.senate.gov/public/index.cfm?FuseAction=Hearings.Testimony&Hearing_ID=1534&Witness_ID=4344.]